Life is a journey, one with many open doors, most of which we manifest. Room 32 reveals and reminds each of us about our own personal power to take hold of our destiny and live the life we desire. Through accounts of her life, Diane takes the reader under her wing as she shares fond memories, lessons learned, times of pain and struggle, tests of the spirit, and the grace of self-discovery.

Diane's writing unfolds as if layers are being pulled off of fear yet builds upon itself like a muscle growing stronger as she questions life's meaning and her purpose and role in it all. Whether you are asking similar questions or find yourself on a fulfilling path, Room 32 reads like an open heart and welcomes you to explore your own beliefs, values, and dreams.

-Stephanie Soule-Maggio, Marketing Director

ROOM 32

A Memoir

Judy -
you are a
blessing!
Here's hoping you
have more time
space to relax
to enjoy!
Peace -
Diane

DIANE BANASIAK

BALBOA
PRESS

A DIVISION OF HAY HOUSE

Balboa Press books may be ordered through booksellers or by contacting:

Balboa Press
A Division of Hay House
1663 Liberty Drive
Bloomington, IN 47403
www.balboapress.com
1-(877) 407-4847

ISBN: 978-1-4525-5395-5 (sc)
ISBN: 978-1-4525-5396-2 (e)

Because of the dynamic nature of the Internet, any web addresses or links contained in this book may have changed since publication and may no longer be valid. The views expressed in this work are solely those of the author and do not necessarily reflect the views of the publisher, and the publisher hereby disclaims any responsibility for them.

The author of this book does not dispense medical advice or prescribe the use of any technique as a form of treatment for physical, emotional, or medical problems without the advice of a physician, either directly or indirectly. The intent of the author is only to offer information of a general nature to help you in your quest for emotional and spiritual well-being. In the event you use any of the information in this book for yourself, which is your constitutional right, the author and the publisher assume no responsibility for your actions.

Any people depicted in stock imagery provided by Thinkstock are models, and such images are being used for illustrative purposes only.
Certain stock imagery © Thinkstock.

Printed in the United States of America

Balboa Press rev. date: 2/22/2013

When I dare to be powerful—to use my strength in the service of my vision, then it becomes less and less important whether I am afraid.

~ ANDRE LORDE (1934-1992)

Room 32 is dedicated to my students. I started living and dancing in the classroom. I am most grateful.

A Few Opening Comments

Room 32 is my own creation. It comes from my own life. However, I have decided to change the names of many of the people and places you will encounter in this book in order to be sensitive to those who may not want to see their names in print. I also admit this story has a lot to do with my perspective—my own vision. If you ask others, perhaps they would indeed tell you a different story. What was and is true for me, may not have been true for my sisters or neighbors or friends.

Writing and publishing my story is an important part of my journey, and as with all stories I know it will make a difference in the community. However, my intention with *Room 32* is to share my own journey as a way to help others along their own path. We all go through challenges and difficulties in this life, but we are not alone on our journey. There have been others who have traveled the same roads we have traveled.

Furthermore, we have all made errors and taken a few missteps; it is just part of being human. But those errors and missteps are only a small part of who we are. We can all create something out of our darkest hour; we just have to be willing to be transformed along the way, and transformations are never easy.

I hope my story will be a blessing to you, dear reader. May this blessing be one that encourages you, inspires you and helps you to cherish the wonderful life that is uniquely yours to express and to enjoy.

Introduction

We all have a story to tell, one that needs to be told.

Sometimes we tell that story for others, but most of the time we tell our story to make sense of things, to put things in perspective, to understand the "why" behind our actions.

I am telling this story in an attempt to embrace all of me, the parts I like and the parts I don't like. It has been a long journey, but it feels so good to get my story out in the open and to celebrate my life, even if it has been filled with errors and missteps. I have taken many wrong turns and made some poor choices, but my biggest error was this: I looked for love outside myself. I thought someone else could save me, but I did not need a savior. I simply needed to love and embrace myself, flaws and all. When I did this, when I established a deep abiding love for myself and a generous self-acceptance, my world changed. Simply put, I discovered my own power. Today, living from this powerful place is what matters most to me.

My transformation began in high school in Room 32, which was my drama room. In that room, I discovered a place where dreams were indulged, characters created and re-created, and life was a dynamic process born from the imagination. Cultivating believable characters was not an accident. Characters came alive in Room 32 because an actor or an actress could breathe life into the pages of a script and thus transform a platform or a stage into a whole new world.

Hope, my drama teacher and coach, inspired my fellow students and I to engage in a process of becoming, of creating. That process would culminate with a drama performance meant to inspire and entertain, but Hope made it very clear to us that the life of the characters we created did not end with the drama performance. We were instructed to capture only a period of time on stage, knowing, seeing and believing that the story and the life of our character went on even after our final exit from the stage.

In many ways, I want to re-create a period of time in my life for you. However, the story you read here began before the words were written down, and the story continues long after you get to the final pages of this book. This "slice of time" is meant to inform and underscore a transformation that took place within me and around me.

But transformations are intangible and ineffable, and they are hard to capture on paper. That is why "story" seems to be the best way for me to speak about my transformation, about the new awareness that has captured my mind and liberated my heart.

In Room 32, I got a glimpse of this vision: we have the power within ourselves to find our way and make our way in this world. We create our lives, and our lives move and unfold in the direction of the scripts we hold and choose to embrace.

Proclaiming myself as creator has been my greatest victory, my brightest achievement, for I am at the center of my life—my life moves and unfolds in the direction of the "scripts" I choose to entertain. However, most of my life I held on to what I call the "church girl script." Essentially, I gave my power over to the Roman Catholic Church, and I was at the mercy of powerful forces outside myself. The powerful, awesome and transcendent God of the Catholic church overtook me and, at times, was ready to crush me. That was the script I held for most of my life, the vision I chose to embrace and to proclaim.

This story is the celebration of a woman who took the journey within and found her own inner sanctuary, which I call Room 32. Finding an inner sanctuary has liberated me and inspired me to embark on a powerful new destiny.

What will the future bring? Only time will tell. For now, let us take a look at a slice of my life, which I have come to love, embrace, and celebrate as unique—and me. The journey is not over, and I am still in the process of writing and creating the next chapters, but I want to share with you what happened and how I came to discover a deep, abiding sanctuary within me.

I hope the same thing can happen to you, dear reader. I hope that you will find a way to come to terms with your life and your choices—to love yourself and to love yourself fiercely. That reconciliation with yourself is all that matters and once you find a home within yourself, then you can find a home almost anywhere, and anyone and everyone can become your family.

CHAPTER ONE
Spirit Takes Form

I THINK WE ALL HAVE a spiritual purpose in life that manifests itself in different ways. For me, it was a major focus. While my friends and family members were busy sewing, cooking and designing things, I was trying to figure out how I could become the navigator of my life when the spiritual realm and the spiritual world held my attention and captured my mind and my heart. I often wondered why I couldn't be like everyone else.

Like Jacob in the Old Testament, I came out of the womb wrestling with God. I wrestled because deep down I preferred the spiritual world, yet somehow I found myself in a physical form wondering just how I got here and why. This flesh-and-bone existence was strangely appealing, quite exciting, and very mysterious. How to navigate this physical world was my challenge.

The physical awareness of my body set the stage for my wrestling match, and it was at puberty that the match became pronounced. Did I know that I was wrestling with God back then? Probably not. My body was changing, and I was going to mature and develop, to find a way to make a living and to find a husband. However, I often wondered how.

Growing up in a strict, Catholic environment put me strangely at odds with the world. I grew up in a religious world in which the Mass was in Latin, the priest was the religious leader in the community, and he and the sisters made promises: promises to be both obedient and chaste. To emulate the priest seemed the best course of action—at least if you wanted to get God's attention—and if I couldn't be a priest, at least I could learn from a priest, work with a priest, and listen to his every word. In fact, my first job was at my parish rectory. I was fourteen years old and essentially working for the priests. I answered the phone, scheduled appointments, and even served the priests their dinner. If power was centered in the hands of the priests, then I wanted to be with them and work for them. Back then this seemed the best course of action.

Most of my childhood energy was spent at church—contemplating the Catholic church and its traditions and trying to find the right formula to gain God's approval and stay in God's good grace. I wanted to get it right because being in heaven with God was my goal, and the idea of an eternity without God was my greatest fear. For me, growing up Catholic meant you had to watch all your actions and behaviors very carefully; one misstep and I might be living in that fiery pit called hell forever.

Issues of job security or financial stability were pretty insignificant. From early on I believed that if I looked for things such as wealth or fame then, at some point, my soul would be in danger of eternal damnation. In fact, being in business was the most dangerous profession to choose. A business woman was after money. She sold a product to bring in an income. In my mind to directly pursue wealth and a wealthy lifestyle could get you in trouble with the Lord. I concluded that it was best not to pursue money directly. After all in Luke's gospel, Jesus called the poor blessed. If the poor were indeed the blessed ones, then any desires for greatness might put my salvation at risk as well. So choosing a career path that would provide me with just the basics might be the wisest course of action.

On top of this was a deep inner unrest. This unrest developed because for most of my life I felt as if I had no real place to call home, not if "being home" means being at peace with oneself and being relaxed, comfortable, safe, and secure. There were periods in my life when I had moments of peace, comfort, and security, but most of my life I have been a wanderer in a search of a place to belong.

My homecoming has a lot to do with my sexuality and embracing a wild and creative part of myself. Sex and sexuality caught my attention from as a early on. I was a young girl when I first noticed things about men and women—how they interacted, what they said and how they would embrace each other in the most intimate of ways. What to make of this powerful, creative force was part of my quest. Yet once I discovered the power to create, I did not know what to do with it. I did not know that with the power to create came the power to destroy, and that if I used the power God had given me the wrong way, then I would grow to hate myself and live as a stranger in a strange land.

Embracing this creative part of me really began back in high school. Room 32 was the drama room at Holy Jesus High School, and acting and directing classes were held there. When I discovered Room 32 during my sophomore year, everything changed. I tasted something different in Room 32. It was there in the drama room that I was given the space to explore, dream, and experiment with life. At times my fellow students and I wore masks and developed characters for live performances, but it was so exciting to become someone else—to create a believable character who was not me. I loved Room 32 because there I tasted a life that I had not tasted before. There I experimented with myself as a big, creative being.

When you are a teenager and your body is full of desire, a place like Room 32 was the best place to be. I could take all my emotions and channel them in very productive ways. Sometimes I would memorize lines, developing a believable, three-dimensional character. Other times, I worked on one of the many crews needed to make a drama performance "come alive."

Hope, our drama coach, helped the other students and I to realize that each of us had an important part to play in the production of a drama performance. We each were valuable. There were no small parts in Hope's mind; she believed this deep down in her soul. I wasn't always convinced.

Having a big part meant you were one of the focal points on stage, and I loved it. With a big part, you got the audience's attention and could claim stardom, even if only for a moment. This meant I could leave my small life behind, bask in the lights, and take center stage.

In many ways my story is about claiming and embracing this space, a space I still call Room 32. However, it is also about internalizing Room 32 and finding a deep creative voice within me. It has taken most of my life to do this work, to find the space and allow myself the room to expand, grow, and dream, but at least I have "made it." For had I not been able to integrate Room 32 and expand the boundaries of my own existence, then there would be no story to tell, and I wouldn't have much wisdom to offer you dear reader.

My story is personal and confessional. In the pages of this book, you will discover Diane, a woman many people do not know. I can say I hid her very well. Only a few friends, confidants, and therapists know the full story. Now you will know, and this knowledge may help to inform you as you try to navigate this physical world as a spiritual creation.

Had it not been for my coaches, mentors, and therapists, I probably would not have made it to this strange, wonderful, and beautiful place I call home today. My mentors allowed me to be Diane, to come to my own conclusions, to wrestle with my decisions and choices, and to affirm those choices even if they would not have chosen my way of doing things.

I received so much support on my journey, but often I found that support outside the institutional church. There were certainly mentors and guides within the church who were open and able to grant me the freedom to think for myself, but the vast majority of my mentors and guides were those on the fringes of the church, those who had left the church or who did not have the same religious affiliation as I did. I know the church gave me a foundation, but today my home is not restricted to one institution or a certain set of doctrines and dogmas. I am much freer now, and I am grateful.

The journey home is never easy. The path will be rocky and torn by war, and we will have to slay more than a few demons along the way. We also will have to come to terms with belief systems we have inherited from our childhood. As adults, what doesn't fit anymore we must discard, and what works we must integrate into our new vision. We must claim our own power and authority, as scary as that may be. However, once we do claim our power, then we will find the whole world opens up, and our real work can begin.

CHAPTER TWO
The Room with Many Unanswered Questions

FOR THE MOST PART, I enjoyed my childhood and many of my childhood adventures. I played ball out in the street with the neighbors and hide-and-seek around the apartment building with my sisters, cousins, and good friends. My family took weekly trips to Tasty Freeze for ice cream, and my sisters and I played outside on hot summer days in the sprinkler in our backyard. We had a swing set and a picnic table to enjoy, both of which my father had constructed. Life was good, and summers were the best.

Television changed everything for me. As a child, I remember watching the Beatles on *The Ed Sullivan Show* while playing my guitar and singing, "I want to hold your hand." Did I know what those words meant back then? Did I know that holding hands could lead to a kiss or even more? Probably not. But I did know that when the Beatles went on stage, the crowd went wild, and it seemed to me that most of that crowd was composed of girls and young women. What effect did these young men have on these girls and women? Many of the girls screamed, and some fainted. Why? Worse yet, why were my parents worried about me watching these kinds of television shows? What did they know that I did not?

My favorite TV shows when I was a child were tame compared with what you see on TV today. As a child, I liked to watch *I Love Lucy* and *The Dick Van Dyke Show*. Lucy and Desi and Rob and Laura, though married, slept in separate beds. They would kiss on the cheek and rarely on the lips. Of course, I noticed because life was different for me at home. My parents had one bed, and sometimes they did more than just kiss. Yet, when I watched TV, I saw a different story. What was I to believe?

5

One night when was about five years old, I "walked in" on my parents. I didn't know what to do; this was certainly not *I Love Lucy*. Of course, my parents were pretty uncomfortable. Dad didn't explain, but he asked me to leave the room; he got dressed and then comforted me. Sure I was puzzled and confused. Who wouldn't be? But he didn't really say much, and it was like I had stepped into a world that was essentially off limits to me.

I also remember the girl next door who was older than I was. I liked to visit her and chat about life and boys and dating; she had a boyfriend who was tall, dark, and handsome, and I wondered when a boy like that might be mine. I watched my neighbor carefully, wondering why she dressed the way she did, waited for John's phone calls, and enjoyed kissing so much. I was captivated. After all, this was real life, and it was unfolding right before my eyes.

My wondering came to a head when my girlfriends and I (we were probably ten at the time) sat on the lawn outside my house. We were chatting about the birds and the bees. My friend Marie told me that she knew all about sex. I was curious for more information. "Diane, I know about sex. I know what people do to bring new babies into the world. I know how it works and what goes on in the bedroom," she proclaimed.

I couldn't believe it. "Marie, if what you say is true, then my mother would have told me all about this. She hasn't. My mom wouldn't keep a thing like that from me, and I will prove it to you."

I walked away in certitude. Marie had been told some wild tale about naked bodies and parts that fit together in the most intimate way. It all sounded disturbing to me, and I knew my mother would set Marie straight.

I remember when I told my mom what Marie had said. My mother remained calm and cool. "Your friend is telling the truth," Mom said.

"No, Mom No! I can't believe it! How could this be? And you kept it from me? Oh no!"

With this newfound knowledge, I clamored throughout the house. I had essentially been told the "big secret" by a girlfriend and not my mother. I felt betrayed, and I wondered why my Mom had kept this knowledge from me. I was sad and angry and scared. Becoming a young woman was on the horizon, and I didn't like what I saw. I wondered whom could I trust and turn to for guidance in this matter.

CHAPTER THREE
The Room with My Family of Origin

I KNEW SOMETHING WAS WRONG with my family. My Dad's drinking and violent outbursts had a lot to do with it. I wondered why my Dad was so unhappy. He had a good wife, four girls, a good job and a home. What more could someone want? What did he want? Was this his vocation or had Dad made some terrible mistake? Had Dad bargained with God and the deal gone bad?

As a child, I felt uncomfortable in my skin, as if somehow I had created my Dad's world, as if I was responsible for his anger and depression. This heaviness stayed with me for a long time. At times I felt trapped in a rather conflicted existence. Sometimes I wondered if this conflict had to do with my Polish heritage. My Dad was born in the United States, but my sisters and I were only the second generation of Banasiaks to claim Chicago as our home. Did we belong in Chicago, Illinois? Could the United States of America be our new home?

To make matters worse, I was a child who followed rules to the extreme, especially when Mom left me in charge of my sisters. One day, when I was about five or six, I remember our neighbor needed to return a key to my parents, but my parents were away. I still remember agonizing over Jim's request to open the door. "Diane, you know me. It's Jim, your neighbor. Just open the door and I will give you the key," he stated quite emphatically.

I just couldn't open the door to get the key. My parents told me not to open it at all. What part of this did Jim not understand? "Jim, Mom and Dad said not to open the door to anyone—not anyone. I will get in trouble if I take the key from you. I just can't open this door."

I peered at him through the window, wondering if he would understand. Disobeying Mom and Dad could be dangerous. Yet, it all seemed so trivial, and I wondered why I couldn't decide for myself what to do.

For a long time, this story became one of my hallmarks. My family members and I laughed about that story for years, but deep down I realized that it was hard for me to draw my own conclusions when an authority figure laid down a particular course of action. Could I take exception to the rules, and if I did, what would be the cost? Would I be neglected, abandoned or, worse yet, not loved?

Following the rules was important in my household. So I struggled early on to allow myself to think and make my own choices. Mostly, I thought others knew best. My parents, teachers, or church authority figures always seemed to know what was best. If I followed their lead, then perhaps I could be successful or maybe even holy. But if I abandoned their thinking and experimented on my own, anything could happen. When bad things happened, I often concluded that I shouldn't have been thinking on my own. "Just accept what you are told, Diane, and everything will work out in the end," I would tell myself.

Coming from a Polish American family made life wonderfully complicated too. When my parents and I arrived at my grandparents' house each week and my grandmother opened the door, we would step into a time and a place that was distinctly Polish—a world that some knew only by way of a newspaper or magazine.

At my grandparents' home, Polish was spoken, and Polish delicacies were consumed. Polish programs could be heard on the radio, and Polish songs were sung. In fact, when Busia (my grandmother) would break into song, which she did quite often, her songs were sung in Polish. I could listen to the music but couldn't appreciate the lyrics, the sentiment, or Busia's feelings. There was a cultural gap between us, and I couldn't seem to bridge it. I could only watch and listen and wonder what was going on and why she was singing with so much joy and enthusiasm.

It wasn't until adulthood that I understood that my sisters and I would be the first generation to really gain a foothold in this new land. We would be the beneficiaries of my grandparents' decision to leave Poland and journey by ship to a new and strange land. Would my sisters and I make it? Would we be successful? Only time would tell, but even we, the second generation of Americans, would have obstacles and challenges to overcome.

Growing up as the grandchild of immigrants made life beautifully complex. I existed in two worlds, trying to navigate two places at the same time. Belonging was something I wanted and something I know my Dad desperately wanted as well, but belonging came with a price tag and often that meant abandoning the customs and the culture that were familiar and embracing a new world which was exciting, strange, and ripe for exploration.

Belonging is a process, not unlike learning to dance, and once I figured out the steps and understood the rhythm, life started to make sense. But in puberty, life would not make much sense. In puberty, I would enter another world, and I was not prepared. No one really warned me about what would lie ahead and what would be a natural part of my maturation. I essentially had to figure out the dance on my own with no partner and no knowledge of the steps I needed to take. Learning to glide across the dance floor would take up most of my life, but I was very hopeful that one day I would glide and others would indeed take notice.

CHAPTER FOUR

The Room of Deep Desires

MY GREATEST CHALLENGE IN LIFE was this: how to reconcile my great bodily needs and desires with my strict religious tradition that allowed no room for exploration or experimentation. I wanted to claim myself as both spiritual and sexual, but how could I? It appeared that I had to pick one or the other.

Once puberty set in and my body started to change and develop, I was frightened and often disturbed. No one had an honest discussion with me about what would happen to me or what I might feel and think, and my Christian tradition gave me little room to explore my sexual identity. I was told early on, however, that being a married woman would allow me to explore my sexual identity or fully develop my sexual self. But what happens if your body is on fire and you are only fifteen, you have no dating partner, and marriage seems like some kind of dream or fairy tale?

I was born into a very zealous Catholic community where sins of the flesh were real and admonished. Even if no one talked about sex and sexuality, everyone knew who were the good girls and who were the bad girls, and I so wanted to be a good girl. But how was I supposed to be good during puberty when sex and sexuality took up more of my consciousness then the rosary or the Catholic Mass?

And in my Catholic world sex was for procreation. I had to be "called" to a married vocation and then, and only then, in a committed union could sex be healthy and holy. Experimenting with sex outside of marriage meant I would be willing to jeopardize my salvation and essentially go toe-to-toe with the big man upstairs. Was I willing to do that? After all, God and the church held all the power for me back then. If I wasn't careful and became too powerful, then I could be destroyed. God did it in the Bible; surely God could and would strike again if the circumstances were right.

Furthermore, the most significant woman in my life at the time told me she never allowed a man to touch her until after her wedding reception. But I wondered, what if I wanted a man to touch me? Would that be so criminal? Would the idea alone send me to hell?

Had I not been such a thoughtful person, somehow I knew my life would be easier, but as a young teenager, how could I become the rebel? Hell was staring me right in the face, and it was not part of some giant pleasure cruise either. In hell there would be the gnashing and grinding of teeth! At least this is what I was told.

I did no personal exploration as a young teen. I didn't like to see my naked body, would not touch myself, and I did not feel very connected to my body. Yet within me I felt deep and often conflicting emotions, and I had thoughts I would not share for fear of damnation.

I also noticed the male anatomy in ways I had not before. I found myself staring at men's pants, wondering what was behind the denim or corduroy exterior. In junior high, most of my teachers were male, and this made for some interesting classroom experiences; I had thoughts and feelings that both excited and disturbed me at the same time, and the attention I received from these male teachers made me feel so good. The classroom discussions about current events and literature were so much better with attractive men leading the way.

Unfortunately, my thighs were growing. I distinctly remember looking down at my thighs, which were starting to take shape in ways that made me feel fat and unattractive. Would these thighs be the obstacle to a future marriage proposal? Would my thighs grow together to become one large mass? Would I have to run away to the circus? Worse yet, how could I ever become the sexual being I hoped to become if I had no one with whom to express myself?

However, it was not only my growing thighs but my underdeveloped chest that was an obstacle. As my girlfriends bought bras for support, I bought a bra to appeal to God to give me what I knew would make me more attractive and desirable: breasts! Would God come through? After all, how could a man be attracted to me if I had underdeveloped breasts? What would I have to do?

Those early years of puberty made me so tense. My objective seemed so far away. Finding a man when I had no breasts and big thighs felt like climbing Mount Everest. Victory would never be mine.

On top of all this was the Roman Catholic tradition that had helped to form and shape me and give me a sense of identity and purpose. As a teenager with very little church history to draw from, I thought about all the great figures in Christianity, including Jesus, who gave up their sexual selves for a bigger, better cause. Perhaps they had achieved a state of perfection that was beyond me, and if my job in this life was to follow in the footsteps of Jesus, how could I do so with such great sexual urges and needs?

In addition to my concerns about my body, I had an often insatiable thirst for God. I loved going to Mass and praying. I loved going on retreats and spending time in contemplation. I was one of those weird church kids who found communion in church rather than on the playground or some friend's basement. And in the back of my mind was the story of the blessing the priest gave when I was still in my mother's womb. Why was I blessed? What did that blessing mean and could the priest take it back?

As I grew older, I began exploring my sexuality with boys whom I found interesting and attractive, and those experiences were encouraged by girlfriends who had pretty much given up on the church. These girlfriends were the true rebels, and I would try to follow them instead of Jesus. However, as I started to give into the desires of the flesh, I began to feel as if I was lying in bed with the Devil and eternity with God was in some kind of strange and different universe.

CHAPTER FIVE
The Room with My Role Model

WHILE MY PARENTS HAD NUMEROUS friends—some of whom my sisters and I had met and some whom we knew through pictures, my Mom's friend Renee stood out to me. Renee went to high school with my mother and was part of her bridal party. But unlike my mother, who took on a traditional 1950s-style role for a woman, Renee would not. In high school, Renee decided she wanted to become an overseas ambassador. Can you imagine? Renee wanted to live outside the United States by pursuing, what seemed to me, an amazing career, and one day her dream came true.

Occasionally, we would receive postcards from Renee. She would let my Mom know what life was like in Bangkok, Thailand, and what adventures she had encountered. Yes, Renee was living on the other side of the world. It's funny: I don't recall ever meeting Renee, but the stories and the postcards captivated me. Renee's life was one grand adventure. What desires took Renee to Asia to explore another world?

Today, looking back, I realize that I wanted to be like Renee. I wanted a world marked by grand adventures and trips around the world. But as a teen, how could I articulate this? How could I reach deep inside myself and say, "This is what I want!"

To claim what I wanted was a very foreign idea. I carried around a long list of expectations, what other people wanted from me and for me. These expectations weren't always spoken, but I knew they were there. So how could I just claim a different life for myself? How dare I?

My father wanted me to be a doctor or lawyer. He wanted wealth and recognition for me and for our family. However, I wasn't in love with science, and being a lawyer had no appeal to me. So it seemed that choosing anything less than these prominent occupations would disappoint my father.

My father was not unlike other first-generation Americans. He knew what it would take to carve out a life and a future, and he knew that you couldn't do it without wealth or prosperity. That is what he really wanted for me. He wanted me to have an easier life, but I feared money. I was afraid that money would corrupt me.

I didn't know it back then, but my mother really wanted her daughters to choose a life not unlike her own. My mother loves Mother's Day more than her own birthday. I think this is because being a mother was her big dream, and having children was all she ever wanted. Mother's Day was a reminder of the important role she played in this world and the prominent role she was playing in the lives of her four daughters. But I was not sure I ever wanted to be a mom. When I considered adventures, motherhood was certainly not on the top of my list. Most of my life, I have been grateful for my mother's decision to bring me into this world, but it was hard for me to carve out a life for myself with my parents' expectations of what a successful life should be.

If Renee had been my mentor and role model, then I am not sure if my story would continue as it did, but Renee was more of a figure in a fairy tale than a real human being. And although Renee was in Asia having grand adventures and exploring a different culture, I was on the south side of Chicago trying to figure things out while juggling the many expectations of what I should do and who I should become.

Sure I danced as a teenager, but dancing through life was meant for people like Renee and movie stars and celebrities. Polish American Catholic kids from the south side of Chicago were encouraged to be practical, make wise choices, and consider the sacrifices of their ancestors.

CHAPTER SIX
The Catholic Room

GROWING UP CATHOLIC GAVE ME a feeling of safety and security. I knew where I belonged and to whom I belonged. I turned to God—especially Jesus—on a regular basis to ask for guidance on how to navigate through life, and, of course, to ask for forgiveness from sin. The Trinity was my spiritual family from the very beginning. Early on, this all made sense to me, and the doctrines and the dogmas just a part of the Catholic tradition.

Sometimes I would tell those outside my tradition that growing up Catholic was a lot like growing up as a Polish American. Could I do anything about my ethnicity? No. So could I do anything about my religious affiliation? No. I often felt that being Catholic was simply a part of my identity. Could I evaluate some things, such as whether to go to confession regularly, and weigh alternatives? Sure, I could. But to leave the Catholic faith for a new religious home was just not conceivable to me when I was younger. There was no life apart from the Catholic church. This meant that sometimes I might protest, but I had better not leave my Catholic home.

One of my good friends was Lutheran. She attended Protestant services that were different from my own, and in the summer her church organized a vacation Bible school for all the kids in the neighborhood. I enjoyed the Bible school, but I never joined Sherry; I never became Lutheran. Sometimes I really wanted to join Sherry. We had so much fun at her vacation Bible school, but something always held me back from taking that step with Sherry. Perhaps it was our rituals and our traditions as Catholics.

Being Catholic had meant following ancient rituals and an ancient tradition. These rituals and that tradition went back to Jesus and the Last Supper.

Who else could claim such a holy connection with our ancestors and with Jesus? After all, we had the eucharist; the little wafer actually became the body of Jesus when the priest consecrated it. No one else could consecrate the eucharist except the priest. He had a privileged position in our church community. In fact, as a little girl I was told that not only was the priest consecrated, but so were his fingers. Only he could hold the eucharist.

When my sister Karen and I made our First Holy Communion in 1967, we were excited and full of anticipation. What would it be like to consume the eucharist? How would Jesus change us? Would he? For this special event we received beautiful white dresses. They were embroidered with lace trim, and they sparkled in the light. I never wore anything so beautiful. Those dresses made me feel that Karen and I were princesses, and of course we were. We were going to receive the body of Jesus. We were going to become part of the Catholic family in a very special way.

Back in 1967 we were the only ones to make our communion that Sunday in May. Karen and I took center stage. Our whole church community watched us that day with great reverence, respect and awe. We were going to hold a privileged place in the community. We were going to have the Eucharist— the Body of Jesus. I still remember that day like it was yesterday. My Dad took pictures of us before and after the service; he had to document this sacred affair, and we had to pose with a look of reverence on our faces. On that beautiful day in May of 1967, we became apart of the Catholic family in a very big way. We were nourished by Jesus. There was no turning back.

CHAPTER SEVEN

Tasting a Different Kind of Existence in Room 32

My FIRST YEAR IN HIGH school, I kept to myself, did my homework, and played it safe. Of course I watched the upperclassmen leading a different kind of life. Some got rides home from their boyfriends. Some rolled up their skirts as they left the halls of Holy Jesus High School, and others smoked on the way home from school. As a freshman, I wondered what these choices meant and what these girls were up to, but I thought it might not be best to follow these upperclassmen.

Holy Jesus High was run by the Sisters of Samuel, and those sisters were strict. Sister Planeda used her eraser as a weapon in class. If you didn't conjugate your verbs correctly, then you would be hit with an eraser. Eraser marks on your uniform were marks no one wanted. It was all very humiliating. It was better to learn those Spanish verbs I concluded.

I also remember some girls had their skits hemmed too high, and this would result in torn skirts and bruised egos to teach the girls at Holy Jesus High a lesson. Of course the rules regarding the length of our skirts did not make us fashionable in the "real world," but the sisters did not seem to care. They had a school to run and important standards to uphold.

I also remember that we were instructed not to wear white at our prom. White dresses could cause boys to think about bedsheets, and everyone knew where that could lead.

But mostly I remember the sisters I had in high school were unhappy. They had jobs to do, but those jobs didn't seem to bring joy to their hearts or smiles to their faces. I often wondered why.

Sister Charity was the one exception. She was our music teacher and one of the most passionate sisters at Holy Jesus High. She loved music of all types, but it always seemed to me that opera was her favorite. How she got us teenage girls excited about opera is still a mystery to me, but somehow Sister Charity did it. In fact, I attended my first Italian opera because of Sister Charity's influence. She made the story three dimensional, and she helped us to develop a real appreciation for each of the many voices who had a part in the telling of the story. But in Sister Charity's class I was a spectator. I was living a safe and comfortable existence on the sidelines, listening to performers take on dramatic roles.

In sophomore year, everything changed for me; I began to get a taste of a different kind of existence. In sophomore year, I entered Room 32 for the very first time. It is hard to describe the room and how it made me feel as a sophomore in high school. But when I walked into that room in September of 1976, my world changed.

Our job as students in Room 32 was to create believable stories and believable characters—to make a play come alive. In Room 32, I was being summoned to create. This had never happened before. I liked the way it felt. My body was alive and on fire, and I had so much to share.

I tried out for a small part in *Stage Door*. I was so excited, but I was also nervous especially when I got the part in this play. I was going to be on stage. I could hardly wait for rehearsals to begin.

Unfortunately, my family did not understand. I ran home with great excitement that day to share my new discovery and this wonderful new opportunity, but my family did not share my enthusiasm. "Why don't you want to be here with us?" my Dad inquired.

"Dad, this is something alive and real and new to me. I think I can do something in Room 32 I have never done before."

My Dad just stared at me, wondering what had gone wrong. I couldn't convince my Dad that everything was fine. We were in two different worlds at that moment with what seemed like an ocean between us and each of us with no way of getting to the other side. My Dad was just not sure how this experimentation could help me with my future and a successful career.

I would be spending more time after school, staying later for rehearsals and taking the late bus home. As a result, I would begin to separate myself from the rest of my family, a natural course for a teenager. But I was the only Banasiak who wanted to experiment in Room 32, the only one who seemed to want more than her home life could offer. Why was this the case for me? Why couldn't I be content with what I had at home?

Hope was the drama teacher at Holy Jesus High, but she was not like the rest of the teachers in the school. She was single and living outside the convent. She smoked cigarettes and enjoyed a glass of wine on occasion and dated men. And Hope wanted all of us to call her by her first name, which we did with pride. Hope was also an accomplished performer, and she was teaching all of us girls how to emote. Hope seemed happier and more adjusted to life as a high school teacher than some of the sisters. And because Hope was our leader in Room 32, she set the tone for life there.

Time spent in Room 32 was very different than anywhere else in the school. First of all, there were boys in Room 32. Holy Jesus High was a private, all-girl, Catholic school, but in Room 32, we had boys visit us; they would come from neighboring schools and try out for male roles in our drama performances. For a teenage girl this was amazing. I didn't have to go very far to go to talk to a boy. Also, as long as we did not smoke in the building, Hope did not care if we took a cigarette break between scenes. And when the theater was dark and no one was watching, girls were known to make out with their boyfriends right in the auditorium at the school.

My friends in Room 32 enjoyed very expressive and creative art forms, which included theater, dance, and music. These theater people were wildly exciting to me because they gave themselves over to a process that was hard to explain to an outside observer. Forming a character, a voice, another life takes effort and care. You have to let go of who you are to become someone else. Becoming someone else took my breath away. Perhaps if I could literally become someone else, then I could explore a world that was essentially off limits to me.

Back then, I did not realize I was doing this. But today, I realize that in Room 32—a room in a private, all-girls, Catholic high school—I was given the permission to explore. Breathing was easier in Room 32; there I could create the Diane I wanted to become!

CHAPTER EIGHT

A Room at the Starkowski House

MARGE STARKOWSKI WAS MY BEST friend when I was in high school even though she went to public school, and I went to a private school. Public school was not an option for the Banasiak girls. Attending a Catholic school made the most sense to my parents, even if that decision meant we couldn't afford family vacations or big summertime adventures.

At Marge's house I felt more relaxed and at ease. Things were not always neat and tidy there, and I liked that. Having the freedom to let things go was so foreign to me. My Mom and Dad wanted the house in order every day.

With seven children under one roof, the Starkowski family had to be practical. Religious education had its place in their home, but the practical matters of living, including maintaining a home, finding a good career, and caring for children, were part of life for the Starkowskis. In fact, when Marge started to work as a young girl, saving for the future was already on her mind.

Also, dirt and dust and a cluttered home were not obstacles in the Starkowski household; they were just part of life. Marge and her sisters and brothers had chores every weekend, and many of those chores involved cleaning different parts of the house. Once a week the house was orderly again. However, during the week, this family of nine had to accept the way things were. Everything and everyone couldn't be in order, and everything couldn't be kept neat and clean every day of the week.

I experienced a great freedom at Marge's home. Going to Marge's house meant I could relax a little and accept "the way things were." It was okay to be messy, and being creative often demanded quite a mess, whether the Starkowskis were creating a meal or a new dress. Messiness was not enemy in the Starkowski household.

I loved being with Marge and her family, but on the way back home, I would find that her practical world, though very comfortable and real and lovely, was not the world I could claim as my own. I had a "big" job to do in this world. What it was, was a real mystery. But an ordinary life just didn't seem within reach. I felt I had something big I had to accomplish, and the weight of that mission often felt more like a burden than a blessing.

At Marge's house, I could just be Diane. I didn't have to indulge that mission or think about my role in this world. I think that is why I kept going back. It felt so good to "just be Diane" because just being Diane seemed good enough!

CHAPTER NINE

The Room with Boys and Dating Partners and Prayer

IN MY THEATER CIRCLE I found boys to date—boys who were actors and musicians and even scholars. I started to get dates with the popular guys, those who had some skill in the performing arts but many who enjoyed the life of the mind as well. They were boys who were living larger lives.

I began to see myself giving over to that piece of myself that hungered for self-expression, but in doing so I was at odds because I was risking being labeled in ways that would be hurtful and demeaning to me. Was I becoming a "bad" girl? Was I "easy?" Did boys start to like me because they knew that I wanted to express myself? And what teenage boy really wants love? Boys had needs that were so primal, so savage. Girls tried to keep things "under control," but it always seemed that boys could hardly do so. Perhaps it is their biology. I am not sure. But I do know that I was intrigued and frightened by the urges boys had. They seemed so different from my own.

Although my parents wanted me to hang out in groups rather than spend time alone with one dating partner, I found ways around this, and before I knew it, I was alone with a boy headed to a rock concert. We made out after the concert, but it was nothing dramatic, and I began to learn new and interesting things about myself. I enjoyed being alone with a boy; I liked to be held and kissed and wondered what sex was really all about.

Losing my virginity didn't happen in a flash. I contemplated what the future might look like if I took such a dramatic step, but I knew I just wasn't ready—until a rock star entered my life.

Don was one of the stars of our drama troupe—at least that is what I saw back then. Don played the guitar, had a great voice, enjoyed theater, could emote, and he was from a divorced home. It is strange to speak of him that way, but I knew very few people who were from divorced homes, and Don was such a rebel. He was wild, had so much freedom, could define his life even as a teen, smoked pot and tobacco, and he would even get the leading role in our plays. To date Don and be his girlfriend meant that either I had "arrived" or that I was really on the path to hell. And Don was so experienced in sex. This I found out rather too quickly.

I never wanted to engage in sex as a teenager and knew in many ways that I wasn't ready, but when my good friend Debbie told me that Don really loved me, I just felt like I had to give in, and I did. Love is what I really wanted. Was sex the key to real love? If I engaged in sex, then would love be mine? Caught up in this emotion and the thought of an endless supply of love, I decided to give in and take a step with Don—a step that would change my life forever.

But having sex was all about keeping Don's love. Back then, his love meant everything to me. Yet having sex was so uneventful. Was this what it was all about, I wondered? If so, then everyone was wrong. This was nothing to brag about and nothing to talk about. It was lifeless for me. Yet on that day, I knew I had entered new territory, an adult world. What to make of this adult world was my new quandary.

I must admit that I wasn't fully present when I had sex with Don, and once it was over, I realized the love would be over just as fast. Shortly after that first encounter, Don broke up with me, and with the breakup things really changed. The feeling of being used stayed with me. Either Don had lied or love was a game I wasn't sure I wanted to play.

Right about this time, prayer started to make sense and become an established practice in my life. With my emotions in flux, prayer centered me and calmed me down in a way that nothing else could. I began to notice that after my prayers had ended, I felt relaxed and more at ease and able to respond to people and situations differently.

Sometimes, however, it was hard for me to quiet myself to pray. Too much negative self-talk often prevented me from praying. But when I did pray, I would experience a great peace within myself and feel much more capable, confident, and at one with the world and myself.

Sometimes praying was difficult because of my choices and decisions. It was hard to quiet my mind, but other times I began to enjoy prayer and looked for more opportunities to connect with God. Growing up Catholic meant that prayer was part of our everyday experience, but as a teen I started to find some value in this practice—value for me. Back then, I did a lot of talking to God. At night, under the covers, I would talk about my day and discuss some of my troubles and challenges. I was told God listened to every prayer, so even if my prayers were quite common and not very elaborate, I knew God listened! Praying was always a great way to end the day, to put things in perspective, and to let things go.

CHAPTER TEN
Wandering from Room to Room

THE YEARS BETWEEN MY DAYS at Holy Jesus High School and my college days at St. Claire were the most difficult for me. I had not established a sense of identity; I was Diane on paper but up for grabs everywhere else. I was in between childhood and adulthood, wondering if I would even make it to the other side.

My fragile emotional life got in the way of everything. I was confused, lonely, and frightened most of the time. Of course, most people did not know it. I hid behind a smile that said, "Everything is alright." Underneath the smile was a fragile girl who was looking for someone to take care of her, love her, and make everything just fine.

Unfortunately, as my high school career came to an end, I developed a very bad case of acne. There were times when my face looked like a war zone. I had blemishes everywhere. Until that time, I felt I had a pretty face and a good smile. The acne changed all that. Worse yet, where would I go to find treatment? Since I was getting older, I was essentially on my own in search of the right doctor. I had appealed to my cousin Mike, who had the same problem as I did. Later I would discover that Mike went to a quack, but this was after my face had been poked and prodded and left bleeding on more than one occasion.

Girls who worked in cosmetics at Marshall Fields promised to help me find a solution and to find beauty. "Have you tried our products?" they asked me. The question came out of nowhere as I was combing my hair in the restroom. I wanted to say, "Who asked you?" But instead I responded, "No, I haven't. I will stop by and check them out."

What was I saying? What was I doing? Cosmetics on my face would only mask the truth; I couldn't cover up the acne. I was certain the coverup would simply make matters worse. That day, I began to think that being beautiful was only for models and Hollywood actresses.

As a teenager, beauty was just as hard to come by as love because I had no sense of my own beauty. I looked for others to affirm my beauty, to validate me. Only by dating attractive boys could I too be called beautiful. The more attractive the dating partner, the more attractive I was; at least this is what I started to believe.

But I also discovered that beauty could be attained by communion with God. So perhaps if my face and my body wouldn't assure me of being physically beautiful and if dating an attractive man was out of my reach, then perhaps I could be beautiful my communing with God and devoting myself to the spiritual life. I started to take this path more seriously, attending retreats, meeting with the sisters, and devoting myself to more prayer and contemplation.

Right after my high school graduation, something erupted inside of me, and all my emotions got the best of me. I broke down in tears before my mother. "Mom, do I have to go to college? Do I need to get a degree?"

My mother was so kind and caring that day. "Diane, I will love you no matter what you do. If you don't want to continue your education, then don't. My love for you will still remain."

That day I was given a freedom, not unlike the freedom I had found in Room 32. My Mom had given me permission to take some time off and "just be." Of course, I would get a job and pay for my living expenses, but I couldn't let go and take the time off to dream and to wonder. I wasn't going to college. What would become of me?

The freedom I was afforded was strange—a mixed blessing. Once I got it, I did not know what to do with it, and all my friends were college bound. They were going on to bigger and better things, and I would take another path. I would get a job as a bank teller in downtown Chicago. I would go to work every day, manage customers' accounts, count money, and balance my teller drawer. My friends, who were serious academics and very talented students, would begin to map out a future for themselves.

Yes, I sat in the same classes with those gifted and talented students, but I never saw myself in the same light. Sure I had a pretty good GPA, but I was directionless. As my friends were getting on with their lives, I worked as a bank teller—going nowhere.

Unfortunately, back then I also compared myself with others, and too often I didn't measure up. I was so hard on myself. My self-talk often tore me in two. I didn't need anyone to belittle me; I could do it all by myself. So staying home from college that first year didn't give me peace and space and tranquility. Staying home meant I was a failure, and perhaps I would never amount to anything. Everyone else I knew had big career plans and goals, and I was counting money and balancing my cash drawer. Everyone else had something going on, and I was still at home living with my family. On the outside looking in, I sat counting money, wondering if I could ever have a big, bold life too.

CHAPTER ELEVEN

A Room at the University

AFTER ONE YEAR AT THE bank, I followed a good friend to Hail Mary University. How did I make my decision? Well, I truly believed that Ann knew what she was doing. She had it together. If I followed Ann to Hail Mary University, then I knew I might make it. Hail Mary University just had to be the next step for me.

Hail Mary University was such a big school, and I knew almost from the beginning that my friend's choice would not work out for me. She liked a big school with sororities and campus parties, but the sororities and parties didn't mean that much to me. I just wanted to belong, to find my way, to get comfortable in my own skin. Hail Mary University couldn't do that for me. Actually, no one could do that for me.

During my first and only semester at Hail Mary University, I remember going to visit Father George, whom I respected. In fact, I was in his class that first semester, and I thought if I went to see him, then perhaps he could provide me with guidance and direction. I sat in a chair beside his desk that day—a man of letters and much acclaim. But then he asked me something that I found to be peculiar. He asked me for a sample of my writing. He told me he could analyze it and get a better sense of what was going on.

"Diane, this does not look good. I am not sure we can continue. What has happened to you? Perhaps we should just end our session here. I am sorry. This is all I can tell you," Father George said this immediately after he reviewed my writing sample.

"Father George, what do you see? Can you please tell me? I am lost and confused and I . . ."

"I am sorry, Diane. We must end our session here and now," said Father George as he cleared his desk and got ready to leave his office.

What was in my writing sample that caused Father George to react this way? He could hardly speak. A look of terror came over his face, and our time together ended so abruptly. My hopes were dashed. He had nothing to offer—nothing of substance. But he left me with a feeling that something was horribly wrong with me, and I might never find my way.

I had no further meetings with Fr. George. I felt sad and rejected. This great Catholic scholar saw something in me that disturbed him, and I was left to figure it out on my own.

In general, my brief experience in college was shocking and scary. Most of the students in college were living a life I had never known before. Some were giving up their values, their religion, and their virginity for freedom at any and all costs. I was scared of what I saw all around me. I didn't know what to do. On top of all this was the Jesuit priest who told me the early biblical stories were mythic—stories told with profound truth but not true in every detail. I just couldn't embrace the information. I felt so betrayed. Either the priest was right and the stories that helped to shape me as a child were legend and myth or Hail Mary University was not the place for me.

I think more than anything my college experience shook my faith to the core. I dropped out after one semester because I was too frightened of what would lie ahead. Thinking for myself might mean coming to terms with my childhood faith, and how could I do that? I did feel betrayed back then, and I ran home in search of some kind of emotional reinforcement. When I ran home, I got involved in church, hung around with the sisters, and participated in retreats. I was comforted again and reassured. I kept my college life and experiences to myself, thinking that playing by the rules would keep me safe and "at home."

I must say that I knew there was another world beyond my Polish-Catholic environment, my church, and Holy Jesus High School and the priests and the sisters, but exploring that new world felt as if I had to give up my citizenship in the Banasiak family. And because power was rooted outside myself, I had to obey and conform or else. My family had strict rules and codes and behaviors, and I knew that God could get angry and hurt me if I didn't follow these codes. Perhaps I feared not only God's wrath but my Dad's wrath or even my Mom's.

Furthermore, my family wasn't a "happy" family. At least I wouldn't describe them that way. Happiness was what we all wanted, but it was elusive. My parents often talked about happiness and encouraged my sisters and I to find happiness, but I knew I couldn't disregard the the family code, my religion, and the Banasiak way of doing things if I wanted to be happy. Was I willing to step outside the boundaries to find myself and maybe pay the price for doing so? Did I really know any other steps to take or any other moves to make?

CHAPTER TWELVE
Another Room – Life in the Convent

AT A RATHER EARLY AGE, with my great sins and battles scars, I decided to take charge of my life once again; I turned to the Servants of God for redemption and a home. I figured if I gave up men and the desires of the flesh for the rest of my life, then maybe God could forgive me and some of my sexual experimentation. Was I manipulating God or at least trying to do so? Perhaps. Unfortunately, the problem for me was this: I just couldn't stand the thought of an eternity without God.

This time Sister Martha would be my guide. I don't exactly remember when we met or how, but Sister Martha intrigued me. Her great faith and devotion to God and her community were quite striking. She spoke so softly and prayerfully, and I do believe that she loved me. Perhaps it was her unconditional love that made the biggest impact on my life. That love was transformational.

So, when I started looking for a home away from home, how could I discount the sisters and their way of life? These were the sisters I had in grammar school and not the ones I had in high school. These sisters were modern, living without their habits, and they were happy. They were fun to be around, engaging, and willing to deal with deep and substantive matters, many of which others found boring, and occasionally they even drank alcohol—sometimes beer and sometimes bourbon depending on the day and on the celebration. But most importantly, the sisters would commune with God each and every day. They would commune in their private prayer times and their community prayer times at the end of the day. There was something about this communion and this communication that I found breathtaking. They talked to God in what seemed to be the most intimate of ways. Could I do the same thing too? Would God hear me? Could I have such an intimacy with God?

The rhythm of convent life was so beautiful and rich and holy. I was drawn in. There was something about these sacred women at prayer that captivated me. I so wanted to be like them. To be a contemplative back then seemed like the best vocation and the highest calling. But I wondered, could I accomplish such a task? Was I called to this vocation too?

God had been calling me, but to what vocation was not clear. But God's call seemed so frightening, amazing, and deafening. Surely this call of God was leading me to the sisters. Surely, this loving and wild creative source of energy wanted me to be a nun. Only time would tell whether this was the best choice.

The convent, a large remodeled and refurnished building located in Aurora, Illinois, was a beautiful place to call home. The floors were made of hardwood, and a great and rather ornate staircase welcomed each visitor as she entered the house. The ornate staircase would lead to our private rooms, and our rooms were large, comfortable and very inviting. In this covenant, we novices had to discern whether we were being called to religious life. This was our task. This novitiate would provide a quiet setting for us to listen to God's call as it would grow and deepen.

In the convent, we were blessed to have a cellar full of food. It shocked me because at home, food was available but not in those quantities. In fact, I remember having to prepare supper one night and going downstairs to the cellar to explore. I imagined that if there was some kind of emergency in town, the community members would come to the convent. The sisters had lots of food and more than enough to spare.

We also had a pool in the backyard. I could swim anytime I wanted. In fact, when my friends visited me in the convent, I believe they thought I had struck it rich. Where were the sacrifices they had heard of? Neither of my friends had pools. They never knew such luxury. I felt very safe and comfortable and even pampered in the convent. Would this be the life for me?

In the convent, I had my own room and a car at my disposal, should I need one. I never had my own room while growing up and never an air-conditioned room. I always had to share a room—sometimes with all three of my sisters.

And in my house, if you wanted air conditioning, then you slept downstairs with the entire family in the family room. There was no space for me at home—or at least that's how it felt.

The space afforded to me in the convent was amazing. I could be with my thoughts, my prayers, or God for hours on end. I was so excited about my new space yet at odds with myself. Did following God mean living in luxury? And if I stayed, would I be able to relate to the ordinary person in the pew? What would I have in common? I was told that in religious life, one's basic needs were cared for so that he or she could devote time and attention to the spiritual life. But I felt like a thief or a parasite—someone who would be living off the good fortune of others.

Furthermore, I think I was just following Sister Martha. She seemed to believe in and support me. She seemed to understand me. But was I just going to the convent to follow her promptings and suggestions and emulate her way of life? Did my love for Sister Martha and her love for me bring me to the convent?

Perhaps I also wanted to be a virgin again and start over. Perhaps I wanted the sisters to absolve me in a way that no priest could. I am not sure. But I did know back then that if I left the convent, I would be on a more difficult path. In those early years, I always thought the difficult path was the better one. Somehow God would be proud of me if I did it all on my own. I tried to convince myself of this fact.

Even though the sisters had all their material needs met, their sexual needs seemed locked away, lost, or forgotten. Unfortunately, I was too young to lock away my sexual needs in a convent. In fact, when I went home for a retreat at my parish, something strange happened. I met a boy who was Catholic, who loved God as I did and wanted to live a life that would make both God and his family proud. That summer Henry went on retreat with me along with twenty other teens. We were all wrestling with ourselves and our choices and trying to hear the voice of God in the mix. Henry caught my attention early on, and before I knew it, we were both wondering what that attraction could mean. Was I still called to be a nun or did God have other plans?

I can't say I left the convent because of Henry, but I knew I couldn't stay with all my desires and emotions running wild within me. I couldn't lie and pretend I wasn't human and excited to connect with a man. After a summer, I decided to leave the convent and explore another significant relationship in my life. I left before I could make any real progress with the sisters and with a religious vocation. In fact, I remember feeling that if I wanted to explore a relationship with a man, then I would have to turn a deaf ear to God. Could I do that? God had been such a great companion for me. If I turned my back on God, then what would lie ahead? I also wondered if Henry and I could have some kind of meaningful sexual expression, perhaps even a holy expression. Would a marriage to Henry make that happen?

CHAPTER THIRTEEN
Settling into a Room in Aurora

AFTER A YEAR AS A bank teller, a semester at Hail Mary University, and a summer in the convent, I decided that I had better grow up and settle down for awhile. If I didn't want to become a nun and I wasn't ready for college, then perhaps I should return to work, get a place of my own, and take steps toward adulthood. So I enlisted the support of some of the parishioners at Holy Angels in Aurora who helped me to pull things together. It would take a few months, but before I knew it, I would be out on my own.

I found a job as a bank teller at the Grand National Bank in Aurora. I was so grateful. Luckily for me, I could get a job as a bank teller pretty easily. I loved working in the lobby at Grand National. The lobby was old and elegant and constructed with marble and wood. I felt so important working at Grand National, like I had arrived. And I had a teller draw full of money for which I was responsible; I felt well respected and trusted.

My first apartment in Aurora was on the second floor of the home of an elderly couple on New Vision Drive. On New Vision, I was starting to grow up and develop a life for myself. Sure my parents were worried, but I was their oldest child, and I was stubborn and determined to make a go of it.

Henry came to visit me in Aurora. We would date and eventually there would be a marriage proposal, but when I saw the way Henry would drink and his violent outbursts, I was frightened. Was I going to repeat the life I saw at home? Was I going to marry someone just like Dad and repeat the life I was trying to escape?

Breaking up with Henry was so hard to do, but it was either break up or say good-bye to a future of happiness, one I was starting to believe in. Henry was so angry the day we broke up. I can still see his red face. I can hear his voice and see his fists. In fact, I thought he might strike me, hurt me, but luckily he just left in a fit of rage.

Henry was gone, and I was alone in Aurora. I was sixty miles from home, about twenty years old, making about $8,000 a year and wondering if I had a future and what it would be. Could I move beyond the circumstances of my home life and my upbringing? Would I beat the odds or would I be just another statistic whose dreams were never realized and whose life ended in poverty and squalor?

CHAPTER FOURTEEN
Challenges in that Room in Aurora

Things changed pretty dramatically in Aurora. I was essentially on my own. I worked forty-plus hours a week, managed my own finances, developed a relationship with a new church community, and began building friendships with my colleagues who were also bank tellers. My family was close enough that I could catch a train home for a short visit, yet they were far enough away that I began to establish my own life. I didn't have a car because I just couldn't afford the expense, but I had a nice apartment, a good job, and a community I grew to love. But I still experienced challenges.

One of my first challenges came from a colleague. I still remember the day Jim came to see me. Jim wanted to talk to someone he could trust about something rather important. He knew that I attended church each week, and he felt I could be trusted. That afternoon he came over to my place for a chat.

I had often taken on the role of counselor or coach with my friends, family members, and colleagues. Sometimes I was surprised by this. What did I know? I was a human being trying to find her way in this world just like everyone else, but sometimes people would seek me out because they saw things in me that I could not see clearly in myself. This was one of those times.

Jim was gay and wanted to know about his future and what he could expect from God. What did I know? I was only twenty, no longer a virgin and just getting started with a life of my own. I knew what was in the Bible, and I knew what was expected in the church world if you followed Jesus, but here was Jim in my presence struggling with himself, his needs, and his future. To be honest, I am not sure if I made much sense that day. I was more concerned with reminding Jim that he was loved by God. I couldn't judge his life. Who was I? And I didn't want to shame him or confuse him or make him feel as if he was not good enough.

Jim and I developed a friendship and a good one, but that friendship changed me more than it changed Jim. I came to realize what a wonderful person Jim was. I got to know about what mattered in his life, who mattered, and what was valuable for him, and I enjoyed his company. We had many adventures together.

I didn't mention my friendship with Jim to my family members back home. I was worried about what they would think. Would they really understand? Besides, I was on my own now, making choices and friends as adults have to do, and I loved it. I enjoyed supporting Jim on his journey. I loved encouraging and listening to Jim, even if others were not as willing to do so.

However, learning more about Jim was not my only challenge. In Aurora, I also met my first divorced woman. It is funny to even put these words on paper, but this is how I remember it. I grew up in the Catholic world, which required couples to make a solemn promise before God and the entire community that they would love, honor, and cherish each other for the rest of their lives—and even if family members grew to hate each other, those members would not renege on their promise, not even if it killed them.

In my family, we had heard stories about the police being called to our relatives' homes. These calls were not made because of a lost child or pet; calls were made because of concerns that someone was going to be hurt by a family member and usually because that family member had been drinking. I am not saying this was a common occurrence, but it did happen. And in my family taking marriage vows was a sacred contract. Even if it got tough, it was best if a married couple just "stuck it out."

So in Aurora, at a church gathering, I met a woman who was divorced and starting over, and unlike my experience with Jim, I was very unkind and judgmental. At first, I wondered what she had done that caused her to get divorced. Of course I thought she was the one who caused the breakup.

However, we never got into the specific details of the marriage or the divorce. I just remember how weird it was to meet a divorced person. In this case, I almost wanted to phone home to say, "Mom and Dad, the world is different out here. People don't stay together. I am not sure what to make of it, but people get divorced in Aurora, Illinois."

I feel bad that I had these thoughts. I am writing this story as a divorced woman who has often been too embarrassed to tell others the truth. As an adult I realize how messy and complicated life can get. Life isn't a fairy tale where the prince and the princess live happily ever after. Some couples do carve out a wonderful life together, and I am grateful, but others grow up in their marriage and once they do, sometimes they can't make the relationship work anymore. Life just isn't as simple as I'd like it to be. There is more gray and less black and white, and in Aurora, ever so slowly, I was beginning to discover this truth.

CHAPTER FIFTEEN

The Classroom and the Mission

MUCH OF MY FREE TIME was spent at Holy Angels parish. I attended Mass each week, taught religious education classes to children in the parish, and even got involved in the peace and justice group. I loved it. I had rituals that provided my life with a great deal of meaning and purpose, and I enjoyed teaching children. Sometimes they weren't always cooperative, but I liked talking to the children about Jesus and teaching them about the Catholic faith.

During my two years in Aurora, it would become clear that I had a vocation in teaching. I loved teaching, and the children liked to be in my class. Over time I got better at managing the classroom and better at handling the material and developing lesson plans. Holy Angels gave me hands-on experience to experiment with a calling I had considered many times. The only trouble for me was this: how could I teach children if I was a sinner and a "pretty bad one" at that? How could I be called to teach when I wasn't the most admirable person and sometimes made mistakes and poor choices?

This was my big dilemma, a dilemma that I wrestled with for most of my adult life. In my more relaxed moments, I would cry out to God, "What are you doing? Are you that desperate?" God rarely ever answered me. Even though I never seemed to get a clear answer from God, I came to embrace my calling, but deep in my heart, I knew God had better options. I guess I tried to convince myself those better options just flat out refused the offer.

Another dramatic moment was when I applied for a position at St. Joseph's Mission in downtown Aurora. I had heard that a minister was looking for a woman to work in the women's shelter at the mission. He needed someone to be on call at night so that if a guest came in looking for a place to stay, this staff member would be the one to take that call. I had a great interview and eventually got the job. The big perk was the free room and board.

This second job came during my second year in Aurora and was a welcome addition to my life. I would have to handle some difficult situations, develop more skills as a leader, and would be able to save a little money. Making $8,000 a year made it difficult to save, but without having to pay room and board, I knew I could do it. By this time I also had my sights on college again. I was growing in confidence, felt called to be a teacher, and life at the mission could help me move along in the direction of my chosen path.

However, I was given a lot of adult responsibility for a twenty-year-old. I dealt with women who were poor and who were looking for a home—a place of refuge. Some of the women were fleeing abusive relationships, some were substance abusers and still others were making a living in prostitution. I had to counsel women and guide them, all without a college degree and the same life experiences many of them had. It was a tremendous opportunity for me, and I think for the most part that I handled it well. The only real difficulty was this: I was called a papist. Most of the men at the mission didn't really believe I was saved.

Luckily for me, I was well liked by the minister and his wife. They knew I was Catholic and attended Mass. They knew I liked the Bible and believed in Jesus. They knew I came from a religious family and that I prayed regularly. But not everyone at the mission felt this way. This made it hard for me to trust some of my new Protestant colleagues. How was I supposed to convince them that I had a role to play at the mission—that I did belong? How was I to show them I was worthy? What could I do?

There was very little I could do. Some were angry that I had gotten the job. Some said a Catholic had never held that position before me. But it wasn't like the job at the St. Joseph's Mission was my dream job. Who else could they get to do what I would do and for no money, only free room and board? I could understand the hatred if I was living the high life, but I was just trying to carve out a living and hopefully save money to put toward future college bills.

Today, I have put the past behind me, but the divisiveness I experienced firsthand has stayed with me. I recognize that today there is more than one version of Christianity, but it still puzzles me that many who claim Jesus as their Savior and Lord are unwilling to accept those whose version of Christianity differs from their own. If Jesus is the example for the rest of us, then what kind of example did he provide? Jesus got himself killed for his radical beliefs and his love of the outcasts. Jesus' love was so expansive. In fact, I am not sure we really want to follow Jesus today and to love as he loved. It is much easier to love those who are just like us.

CHAPTER SIXTEEN
The Room Where Francis and Claire Lived

I HAD A DEVOTION TO St. Francis. When I say this, I do not mean that I worshipped Francis. I just believed that St. Francis really understood the Gospel. I believed that St. Francis "got it right." His love for the outcast and the stranger was so radical, and he cared nothing about wealth or affluence. St. Francis just wanted to serve others and the Lord. When he discovered his calling, he left everything behind him. He spent much of his life depending on the generosity of others to survive. St. Claire embodied much of St. Francis' vision, and I knew if I followed them my life would be blessed.

Keeping St Francis and St. Claire in mind and my desire to attend a small Catholic college, I began to research an environment that would be right for me. In Joliet, Illinois, about an hour from Aurora, I found a small Catholic college. I could easily get there to visit and meet some of the teachers, administrators, and campus ministers. I was so excited because by this time my confidence was up, and I really believed I could have a future as an academic or at the very least get my college degree.

I had a conversation with several of the administrators and teachers at St. Claire, but my conversation with Fr. Bernard stood out. He was an older gentleman, perhaps in his fifties at the time, a scholar himself, and a Carmelite. He was serving as the campus minister and was willing to take time to chat with me. It was a great meeting. He put me at ease and answered all my questions, but it was his presence that stood out to me. He just seemed comfortable being Fr. Bernard. That appealed to me, and his presence—his authentic presence—sold me on the school that day more than any of the admissions counselors.

When I returned to my work at the mission and the bank, I knew that I would have a future beyond my world in Aurora and slowly I would make my plans and get things in order for the big transition. However, leaving Aurora, even with great plans in mind, was so difficult for me. I was starting to build a life for myself and feel good about what I could offer the world, and now I would have to begin again. I knew I could handle college life this time around, but it was leaving Aurora that was so painful. I was loved and respected in Aurora. People depended on me, and I was good at the work I did. Starting over in academia meant I had to say good-bye.

I recognize now that I did not want to grieve. I often moved so fast to keep myself from feeling grief. I have made so many moves since my early twenties, but it has taken most of my life to accept feelings of sadness and grief. I know now that my happiness and joy have everything to do with my ability to embrace my sorrow and loss; I realize that I cannot have one without the other.

CHAPTER SEVENTEEN

University Life – Room 32 Resurfaces Again

EVEN THOUGH I OFTEN THINK of my college years as very difficult because of some of the decisions I made, I also think of those years as a time of real exploration. As my life had grown and developed in Aurora, so too had my life grown and developed at St. Claire. I would experiment there and in that college environment, something would be born. From tragedy came life—and life abundant. It was a slow process, but eventually I would begin to see myself as someone with gifts and talents to offer. Room 32 may have been just a seed within me, but that seed would start to take root.

At St. Claire, I ran cross country. For many college students this might be a natural course of events, but for me this was a big step. My Dad was great at table tennis and could ride a bike and skate, and he was also pretty good at bowling and horseshoes, but these were not the kinds of sports that were being offered to me in college. But I did like to jog, and the cross country team needed members, so one day, I decided to show up for practice to see what the coach would say. Before long, I was in uniform and part of the team.

I must admit, I wasn't always in the top seven—the seven athletes that would compete in a race. In fact, sometimes I was just an extra body just in case one of our better runners couldn't perform. If this had been basketball, I would have been another bench warmer, but this was cross country and everyone on the team had a part to play, no matter what. I really enjoyed being on the team; it made the adjustment to college that much easier.

And it was at St. Claire that I discovered long-distance cycling. Cheap spring break trips were offered to us by a tour group out of Indiana. Wondering Wheels was in business to provide inexpensive trips to college students who wanted to explore cycling and go to Florida without the excesses that often come with spring break vacations. On this tour, we would have religious devotions every day, pray before meals, and think about cycling in terms of our spiritual lives. The terrain could provide good food for thought, and the Florida sun provided us with the tan we all wanted.

Within a couple days, I was hooked. Forty miles wasn't too much of a challenge. The terrain in Florida is relatively flat. This meant we could feel pretty strong and accomplished after a day of cycling. And it was on my first trip that I heard the tour guides talk about coast-to-coast cycling trips. I could not believe it. The idea of a coast-to-coast tour on the seat of my bike sounded like a wonderful possibility. If I got good at this sport, then perhaps a trip of this kind would be within my reach. The idea drifted in and out of my consciousness and would never leave me.

Along with my athletic accomplishments, I was lucky enough to secure a position as a resident assistant in one of dorms on campus. I was in charge of one floor in the dorm, and this meant I would have leadership opportunities on campus along with free room and board. This opportunity gave me a real confidence boost. I had to handle situations that I had never encountered before. I had to confront girls whose boyfriends had stayed overnight and were found showering in the bathroom the next day. I had to sit by the bedside of one student who had been out partying all night and gotten very ill. In addition to my large-scale responsibilities were my everyday administrative duties; I had to be the one to distribute information about the dorm, hold dorm meetings, and keep things running smoothly.

I loved the responsibility and the leadership. It felt so good to have this position. If the administration could trust me to be a leader in the dorm, then perhaps I was a valuable commodity and someone who would be entrusted with even bigger jobs and greater responsibilities.

At St. Claire I was also given my first big role on stage. The play was *The Wisdom of Eve*, and I played the part of Margo Crane. Now this was a drama and not a big seller at St. Claire, but I had a major part to play, and I made sure to invite my friends and family members on opening night. My friend Bill gave me the greatest compliment. I remember his words clearly and distinctly: "Diane, I never saw you on stage. You really developed a believable character. You were Margo Crane." I couldn't believe it. I had succeeded in creating someone else, and I was good at it.

I also had many opportunities to have conversations and dinners with my professors and their families. This too was a major boost for my ego. In my free time, I spent some of my evenings conversing with some of the great minds on campus. For a young woman from the south side of Chicago who doubted her intellectual ability, these were golden opportunities. However, even with some boosts to my ego and development, I still remember my professors asking me, "Diane, what do you think?"

Thinking for myself was so hard to do. I could recite church teaching or my parents' rule book or even a Shakespearean sonnet, but to think for myself, that was scary. Why couldn't I? What had prevented me? Why couldn't I claim my own truth?

Even with limitations, I found ways to thrive and flourish at St. Claire. I was the big fish in a small pond and so happy that my life was moving in a positive direction toward a future and a career. I wasn't exactly dancing through life, but I did feel more graceful and equipped to make choices and changes and to be a leader in this world. I was already a leader at St. Claire, so perhaps all I needed was time and experience and then I could be a leader elsewhere.

CHAPTER EIGHTEEN
A Room at St. Claire College

IN MY EARLY TWENTIES AT St. Claire College, my rebel side developed because of a deep crisis of faith that somehow erupted within me. Essentially, I started to question God's existence. Was God real? Was God good? Was God someone I was taught to believe in order to follow the rituals and the traditions of my ancestors? I wondered. But the questions I asked myself remained on the blackboard in my mind without real investigation. Asking the questions was so difficult to do and to embrace the answers seemed even more frightening to me.

It is kind of ironic because I was a religious studies major who wanted to cling to her faith, yet I had doubts and questions. Did I take this course of study simply to reinforce my faith, to make certain I wouldn't stray very far from my roots, my upbringing, and what I knew as a child? I wondered.

However, much of my struggle did not continue in a religious studies classroom; my struggle grew in my English classes. Studying English literature challenged me in the most amazing ways. I was reading so many literary giants from the past who had real problems with the church, religion, and even God. And once I added English as a second major, the same creative space emerged for me—the space I had experienced back in Room 32—but this time God was losing. I think for the next few years God became terribly silent in my life, like an old relative whom people talk about all the time but someone you've never met. I went to church and prayed, but it was as if I was living in the darkest of nights, and God was in another universe.

The culmination of my wrestling match with God came in a love affair in college. I met a man who took my breath away. He came out of nowhere and started dancing with me at a dance in the college gym. But his dancing wasn't just dancing; his dancing was seductive. I had never met a man like that before. His energy and power over me was wildly exciting, and he was so handsome. Was the ugly duckling going to emerge right on the dance floor and be swept away by this handsome prince? Yes, even given my experimentation, I was still often too naïve, still believed that some of those fairy tales would come true with me playing the lead role. I have to admit that I wanted the physical contact—the love and the affection—but I didn't really know Jerry, what he wanted, and what he was up to.

I was drawn in by our first encounter. And before I knew it, I was taking steps with Jerry that later I would come to regret. He hardly knew me, didn't want to date me, and he just wanted to have sex. For someone with great sexual urges and desires and no marriage partner, this sounded like a good deal, but when he wouldn't acknowledge me in the daylight and wouldn't get together as normal couples do for dates, coffee, or conversation, I knew I had allowed myself to become something less than a full human being. I knew I was living in sin—kind of peculiar for a religious studies major.

As time went on, I began to sink deeper and deeper into a lifestyle that I didn't want, and eventually I would get pregnant—what would be my only pregnancy. I couldn't even imagine having the child. I just couldn't. How could I go home with no degree, no money, and pregnant? Worse yet, my father's drinking and my dysfunctional household would become the foundational home for the new life growing inside me.

I grew up so angry and resentful that my home was not like the *Leave it to Beaver* home and that Dad's drinking and explosive temper had been the gift of some kind of strange and tormented God. As a teenager, along with my sexual identity, I had to come to terms with my Dad and his choices; back then I wanted no part of him.

I was so angry about growing up as I had and now, as a pregnant woman, I was angrier still. How could I bring up a child in an environment that I was trying to run from? How could I have a life and a future with a family with no resources? I began to realize that to have a baby meant that I might repeat what I saw at home, and I could not do that.

CHAPTER NINETEEN
A Very Dark Room

I SPENT A GREAT DEAL of time in contemplation about what to do with my pregnancy. How was I going to handle this new life growing in my womb? I decided to confide in a counselor and a professor along with some of my good friends at St. Claire. One of my peers wanted to support me and assist me on the journey. His mother had had an abortion, and Tom knew what I did not know. His mother was still trying to come to terms with her decision—a decision she had made many years before. I seriously considered having the child. In my naïve moments, I also thought my friends would be with me through it all and would support me. In moments of delusion and fantasy, I thought if I had the baby, then perhaps I would be the hero and everyone would love me, and I would be okay.

One of my professors played a pivotal role in my decision. He did not make the decision for me, but he helped me to take a look at my options. Was I being naïve to think that others would stop their lives to care for me and a new baby? Would I really get a medal at the end of all of this to congratulate me and tell me I had chosen well? I wasn't convinced that having a child at twenty-four would make much difference, and if I went ahead with the pregnancy, then I would be the one who would have to be responsible for a child.

I started to come to terms with my new future. I would have to parent a new life. How could I do that? Worse yet, what if I inflicted the torment and some of my personal struggles on this new life? What if I damaged this new life by having it? What if the child inside me would curse its life and wonder why I ever went ahead with this decision? Being a parent at such a young and fragile time in my life frightened me. Going home to my parents with this new life was also frightening. If I had felt like a failure before, then how would I feel after I delivered this new life?

When all was said and done, it all came down to the pragmatics for me. What resources did I have and where would I live and just how would I support myself? Adulthood was here; I knew that now. One day I took a good look at myself in the mirror and said, "You are a woman, Diane, and your childhood and those fairy tales have ended. Accept your fate and make the best of it." From that moment on, I knew what I had to do.

Once I came to the decision to have the abortion, I had to find a way to get to the hospital in Chicago. I had to ask one of the sisters to loan me her car. At St. Claire, I was a respected student and a resident assistant, and I could be trusted. So I knew I could ask any of the sisters to loan me a car for the day. However, to get the car, I had to lie; the lie nearly tore me in two. How would I be able to face that sister again with this lie on my conscience?

On the way to Chicago, I contemplated what the future would be like, but it was so hard to do. I was with child and, on the way back, I would be without. Could I handle the emptiness when now I was full? I also never made it perfectly clear to Jerry what was going on. Perhaps I should have had a longer conversation with him? Would he have listened? Would he believe that the child growing inside me was his? I decided that I did not want to hear rejection on the phone, and Jerry always seemed more interested in sex then a relationship with me anyway. Would a baby change all that? I didn't think so. I decided I had to handle this all by myself, and I did.

At the hospital, I met a number of women who were just like me. Some were older and some younger, but we were all in this strange and terrifying predicament together. Our conversations were strange to me, somewhat superficial at first, as if we just met on the bus going home from school or work. We talked about our lives and what we were doing with them, if we were dating or married or unattached.

At some point, the conversation changed. I started to inquire why the women had made this decision and why they were going ahead with the abortion. In some ways, I felt like a reporter on CNN doing the necessary investigations to get the story. But several times I wanted to stop the interview and ask, "Are we really making the right decision? Should we stay or should we walk away?"

But I couldn't be that honest with my questions. I had stuffed all the fear inside, and the fear was churning and I was churning and hoping and praying that I could really go through with this.

One of the women who stood out to me was in her late forties with several children already and who was surprised by this latest pregnancy. She knew she couldn't go ahead with this commitment. She looked exhausted and worn out already, as if there was not much energy left to parent another life—a life that wanted to be born but one that would require she sacrifice the few moments she had for herself each day to nurse and care for it. One more baby, one more mouth to feed and she might crack, or so she said to me.

There was another woman, about nineteen, on her second abortion. I couldn't believe it. I began to stare at her with a look of accusation. It appeared abortion was her method of birth control. *What is she doing?* I wondered to myself.

Holding together some semblance of my ego, I made decisions in the waiting room that day. Some of the women were choosing well; others were not. I was on the jury. *Not all of their crimes are of equal weight,* I thought. Who would deliver the verdict? Surely I could not; after all I was one of the condemned myself. Playing Dr. Jekyll and Mr. Hyde that day, I was not sure who I was or if this was the end of the road for me.

I tried to counsel the women that day just to push back my own feelings of terror, but I am not sure it did much at all. I sat by each woman, listened to her story, and tried to reassure her that she would be okay. I did this for me, not for them. For as the clock was ticking and the hour drawing near, I thought I would dissolve into a pool of nothingness. Once it was my turn, and my name was called, I wondered if I would die too. I wondered who would be left to pick up the pieces. My only consolation that day was this: my doctor would be the one to perform the abortion. I knew I could trust my doctor, and it was because of him that I could let go.

CHAPTER TWENTY
The Room with the Jewish Doctor

A COLLEAGUE REFERRED ME TO Dr. Solomon in Chicago. She suggested I see him because he was a good doctor, kind, gentle, and Jewish. His Jewish background stood out to me; I knew I would feel safe and comfortable with a Jewish doctor. I had heard that many reformed Jews had fewer hang-ups about sex, unlike those in the Catholic tradition. I just knew that Dr. Solomon would understand my needs and desires without any judgment.

From the age of sixteen to nineteen, I went to my mother's gynecologist, but it was strange for me to do so. It was strange to see a doctor whom I couldn't trust, who may not keep my confidences. In fact, after one exam, Dr. Rigid took my Mom aside and indicated to her that I was not a little girl anymore. My Mom was shocked, but we didn't speak about this. She just stared at me. She knew something had changed between us. After all, good Catholic girls only had sexual relationships within a marriage. So when the opportunity came to have my own doctor, I was greatly relieved. I could be myself with my own doctor, tell him what was on my mind, ask questions and not worry about him breaking my confidences.

Dr. Solomon was a wonderful man. He was kind and gentle, and he made me feel as if sex was so natural. And after the exam, I got dressed, and I was invited into his office to talk about anything I needed to discuss. Dr. Solomon made no judgments about my needs and desires. If fact, wanting birth control pills just made sense to him, and he gave me a prescription without any drama or any reservations. I kept wondering if being Jewish had a lot to do with this. Did Jewish people understand sexuality different than Catholics did, and if they did, then what could I learn?

I took the birth control pills for a year. During that time, I am not sure that I had sex at all. I did appreciate the fact that I had fewer cramps, but in general, I did not feel right. My heart felt like it was racing, and other times I felt like I was going to pass out. At some point, I threw away the pills, and I decided to try abstinence again. I tried to convince myself that God wanted abstinence anyway, so maybe I should comply.

Eventually, I asked Dr. Solomon for a prescription for a diaphragm. I thought it would be best if I had some protection. It took some getting used to. I didn't like the diaphragm at first, and the spermicidal cream often irritated me. However, I knew that precautions were necessary, especially if I had sex again.

The night Jerry and I got together, I had forgotten to use my diaphragm. I also foolishly lost track of my cycle. I wasn't aware that I was taking some big risks or even what the consequences would be. I just enjoyed the physical contact, the connection with Jerry. I wanted his touch, his embrace, and the intensity of the encounter. And Jerry was so handsome. I kept thinking that if I wanted such an attractive man, then I would have to "pay the price." I did not know how costly that encounter would be.

CHAPTER TWENTY-ONE
The Room Where My Secret Lies

DRESSED IN A HOSPITAL GOWN and a shower cap, I sat in the waiting room alone, praying: "God forgive me. God be with me."

Just before I went in for the operation, a woman approached me. She was a volunteer and had chosen to be with women like me who were going through an abortion. She was there to hold each woman's hand as she went through the procedure. I know very little about her, and I don't even recall her name, but I do distinctly remember her. Most of the time, I call her Grace because she was literally my saving grace that day. But why was Grace there, I wondered? Why would she intentionally join us? Who would do that? Who would volunteer for this job? I tried to ask Grace a few questions, but she didn't say much. She just wanted to be present with me—with all of us.

My doctor was ready to begin, and he told me what he was doing. But almost as soon as he began, I was wincing in pain. I was trying to choke back the pain and the tears and to keep from screaming, but then I looked at Grace. Her eyes were so relaxed and calm, and her fingers were wrapped around mine with a firm, tight grip, like a mother holds her child's hand when there is danger lurking ahead. I think at some point I passed out. The pain was so great that I just gave in and drifted to sleep.

But I do know this: Grace was my witness that day. Her hand kept me focused on the table, especially as the abortion took place and the pain grew worse. I am not sure I would have survived without her.

My abortion was very painful; I felt like I was being sliced open. I wondered if I would die that day. Would I live to tell the story? I was not sure. Yet beside me stood this woman who held my hand as I cried and shook with terror. Grace stood there without words, judgment, or condemnation. Beside me that day stood a woman who held me in my hour of terror when I could not hold myself.

In the recovery room, the other women and I were all groggy; it was the bleeding. Some of us had bled a lot more than we had expected. Would the bleeding stop?

We were told to remain in the recovery room until the nurse released us. We were in the room for some time. Of course, back then, it seemed like an eternity. And what if we died in that room that day? Who would know? And what would everyone say? Only my professor and his wife knew what I was doing that day, and they didn't even have all the details. They just waited at home for my call. They waited and wondered, and I waited and wondered too!

Eventually, we started to feel better, and as we did, we each got up to splash water on our faces, put on some makeup, and return to the world.

I remember that moment like it was yesterday. I still see my face in the mirror. I see my eyes: deep and dark, lost and searching. How would I recover from this terror? Where could I go now? I came to the realization that makeup could not hide the truth of what I did, of who I really was. This wasn't Broadway, and I wasn't playing a part. I was myself, torn and broken and confused, and I was trying to convince myself that it was the best choice, and somehow I would survive.

CHAPTER TWENTY-TWO
The Darkness Grows

FOR SEVERAL YEARS AFTER THE abortion, I entered a dark period. I dated other men and had a few more relationships, but I didn't really feel anything; I was numb. Too numb. Again, I am not sure people noticed because I was so good at plastering on a smile and wearing it like some kind of merit badge across my face. But I had "died" on that abortion table; my smile was no longer my own!

Over the years, I began to see myself as murderer, but I kept wondering why I wasn't incarcerated, knowing full well that others were incarcerated for murder. How could I be living a seemly normal life when I took a life? How could I go on when I had snuffed out a life? No one told me about this self-hatred and torment. Well, maybe they tried, but I know I didn't hear them. Besides, I thought I knew emotional discomfort; after all, I grew up in an alcoholic home. I foolishly thought I could handle pain of all kinds. But after the abortion, it was hard to love myself again. And if by my action I was essentially excommunicated from the Catholic church, then even if God did exist, I am sure he wanted no part of me.

Therapy started to make a difference, but it was so hard to confide in a therapist. I was sure she would judge me and slap on the letter A (for abortion) on me and send me to the town square. But she didn't. She never condemned me. Never. It was in therapy that I slowly started to take a look at myself and my life and make sense of what had happened in ways I had never done before. It would be a costly, emotional, and very challenging ride, but in therapy I would begin to start to love myself again.

There was something dramatic about admitting I needed help. Sure, I loved to help others, but taking care of myself seemed like a strange and self-indulgent thing to do. Besides, I was very good at hiding behind a smile and an energetic personality; it was the mask I wore very well. Being honest about my loneliness, fears, and sins and all my difficulties was another matter altogether. In therapy, I started to realize that some of my biggest mistakes were driven by my deep loneliness.

I found great joy in making connections with others. The deeper the connection, the better I would feel. But by the time I entered therapy, I felt like my circuitry had gone bad and some kind of rewiring had to occur. I didn't know back then that developing a friendship with myself could be the antidote. I kept looking for love and acceptance and approval outside myself. Luckily for me, a therapist could provide me with the love and acceptance I needed so that I could begin to take the journey within.

Talking about myself and my own needs and desires with someone felt strange and liberating. It was as if deep down in the abandoned well of my existence I was excavating the remains of a broken and shattered self. Looking at pieces of my broken self was hard to do. Was I a living tragedy? How could I possibly produce anything out of the mess I had created? But somehow I knew that if I did not do this excavation work I would never be able to create. The seeds of Room 32 were present on that therapist's couch, but at the age of twenty-five, I was just starting to water the seeds of my existence.

Embracing my creaturehood was often difficult. After all, it was this bodily existence that created this crisis and turmoil for me. How could I embrace this body when it wanted to express itself in ways that the church had deemed evil and sinful? Sure marriage could change all that for me. But what if deep down inside I knew that marriage would not be good for me? What if I was a free spirit who needed a larger life—a life that wasn't traditional and like the norm? Falling in line could be destructive of that spirit, right?

I started to realize there were a variety of dance moves to choose from. Which one would I take? Which one should I take? Could I indulge myself and enjoy? Should I just watch the other dancers and sit along the sidelines waiting for something to happen, to change? I did enjoy watching the dance of life, but for me, gliding across that floor seemed like light years away.

CHAPTER TWENTY-THREE
A Very Unique Kind of Room

IN MY SENIOR YEAR OF college, I had the privilege of taking Sister Vivian's class, "Criminal Justice and Christian Faith." In this class, I would have to compose my spiritual autobiography. I would have to get to the "heart of the matter." What was the truth about me, and could I speak about it? The direction of my life was changing and because of Sister Vivian, I began to grow more contemplative as a human being.

Essentially my class would visit and be visited by people who had been in the criminal justice system. Some were victims, and others were offenders. By listening to them, we were to discern what questions, issues, and problems were capturing our visitors' minds and hearts.

One of the women we met was a victim of spousal abuse. Miriam had been beaten by her husband on more than one occasion. In fact, it was often hard to listen to her as she told her story. At times, Miriam lived in between life and death. How had she survived? Miriam's final encounter with her husband took place when she was thrown through the picture window of her home. After that tragic and painful experience, Miriam knew she had to leave.

When Miriam told her story to us back in the spring of 1986, she radiated with peace and with light. I still remember that day like it was yesterday. The anger and resentment were gone, and she was living a big, bold life with wonderful new opportunities. How had Miriam gone from living in the darkness to living in the light? What transformation had taken place? How had this happened?

The secret ingredient for Miriam was forgiveness. She had forgiven her ex-husband, and she had moved on with her life. It wasn't easy. But she knew what she wanted for her future, and in order for Miriam to claim that future, she had to let go of the past. I remember looking at her face and wondering what magic, what power rested within her. She was a strong woman indeed.

Julia was another victim, but her life did not turn out as well. Julia had lost her son in a barroom brawl in California in 1982. Her son, Chris, had wanted to strike out on his own at a very early age. When he arrived in California, the opportunity he had hoped for vanished; at 19 his life abruptly came to an end. When Julia received the news, there were few details, but Julia was determined to embark on a long and painful journey to understand. She had to get to the bottom of things. She had to do the research herself. She spent lots of time and money to get the answers she desperately needed, but all she had were loose ends.

Julia's decision to leave Illinois and head for California took its toll on her family. She had a daughter who lived in Illinois, and a husband, but during her long and painful journey to get the answers she wanted, she lost her living family members who needed her the most. Julia talked about how her son's death destroyed what was left of the family, but I wondered if she had a hand in that destruction too.

I do not want to diminish Julia's experiences here, nor the crime, but when I met Julia she seemed like half a woman. Life—her life—seemed to be leaving her. The light within her was almost gone.

How and why could these women end up in two different places? They had both been victims of crime. They had the scars to prove it. Why was one so full of light and the other so full of darkness? I wanted to understand. I needed to find the answers.

I found my answers in a book that Sister Vivian had suggested: Henri Nouwen's *With Open Hands.* In that book, I learned about prayer—real prayer—and the posture of surrender. Praying, according to Nouwen, has more to do with letting go than hanging on.

Listening to these women's powerful stories brought up issues of control for me. My life, like the lives of these women, felt rather chaotic, and I wanted to be the one to control people and to control my destiny. Nouwen's book helped me to uncover my controlling ways. Until this time, my prayers had been all about me and what I did or didn't want to happen. I soon discovered I was running from God by trying to take over and run my life myself.

This posture of surrender made a big difference for me. With open hands, I had to just "let go and let God." Letting go was often harder than saying a few Hail Mary's or the Lord's Prayer. Letting go in prayer meant letting go of my clenched fists and letting go of what was. How could I do that? I had often been defined by what had been done to me. In many ways, I considered myself a victim, and I was holding on to my victim status with a vengeance.

With Sister Vivian and Nouwen's help, I started to let go. It was the beginning of real prayer for me. I can't say that I fully embraced my creaturehood back then, but I started to take a look at it. I started to see my frail self as a blessing, as someone who needed God to make things right.

From that moment on, surrendering would keep coming up for me. And with that posture, my weaknesses felt more like strengths, and I thought perhaps God could use me—yes, even me.

CHAPTER TWENTY-FOUR
A Room with the Mighty Mustangs

AFTER COLLEGE, AT THE AGE of twenty-six, I returned to Chicago and to life at home with my parents. The return felt so strange after being on my own for six years. Would I live with them forever? Would I be able to make it on my own?

My first job after moving back home was at St. Alexander High School on the south side of Chicago teaching freshman English classes. I was so grateful when the job first became available. However, the salary was a modest $15,000 a year. Sure I was making a living, but what kind of living? Chicago was not like Aurora or Joliet. The cost of housing was more expensive in the big city, and the thought of living on my own in Chicago on this salary seemed nearly impossible.

St. Alexander was only a couple miles from my family home, so I could take the bus to work. I still had no car; the thought of getting a car back then frightened me. When I graduated from St. Claire, I was $8,000 in debt, and I didn't have much in the way of a savings account. I entertained the idea of taking out a loan for a car, but I thought it was better not to take any big steps until I made sure I could work with the mighty mustangs. At St. Alexander, the school's mascot was the mighty mustang—essentially a wild horse. It always seemed like an appropriate mascot for this all male academy on the south side of Chicago. Not all of the boys were wild, but their spirits were strong and so very powerful.

At St. Alexander, my greatest challenge was working with a department chair who didn't appear to like women and who especially didn't like women who tried to think for themselves. I didn't take the job at St. Alexander with a plan to redesign the high school English program, but I did have some good ideas, and Harold had the strangest system for teaching grammar. I hated it. I loved grammar, and I enjoyed teaching, but Harold's method of teaching grammar had to go.

There was another teacher who really liked Harold's work. She would "take me under her wing," and she would be my mentor. It was good having someone like Sherry to help me find my way, but she was a "yes" woman. I found this out from the very beginning. She encouraged me to follow Harold, and if I did, then I would get whatever I wanted. Harold could be the one to help me in this new world of high school academia, and Sherry made it clear that at St. Alexander I couldn't do it without Harold's support.

Working with Sherry and listening to her made it very clear to me that I would only stay one year at St. Alexander. I could not just follow Harold's lead. I knew he had a doctorate, but I was a recent college graduate with some ideas of my own. I would not work for someone who didn't honor and respect my ideas and insights. After all, I was just beginning to realize that I might have a contribution to make. Of course, I kept this information to myself, looking for the right time to make my exit gracefully. In the meantime, I would work with teenage mustangs in an all-male academy, and I would try to keep my sanity.

CHAPTER TWENTY-FIVE
What I Learned in My First Classroom

WITH THOSE MUSTANGS, I HAD to be mighty strong. I almost felt like a drill sergeant that first year in the classroom. I often felt uncomfortable as a teacher; those mustangs were mighty difficult to control.

I still remember when one of my colleagues resigned midyear because it was just too much for her. She was a small, delicate woman and definitely no match for the mustangs. Those mighty mustangs had reduced her to tears on more than one occasion. I was determined that I would not leave St. Alexander as my colleague had left. I didn't want any drama. As a result, I became a difficult and very demanding teacher, and I tried not to smile until I had the reigns firmly in my hands. Trying to break in these mustangs would not be easy, but I knew I could find the strength to complete the job and honor my contract that year.

What I learned was that the "less aggressive" mustangs found home away from home in my room. In fact, one of the teachers would make this comment: "The 'special' boys like to hang out with you, Diane!" Special? Of course, we spoke in a code back then. After all, this was 1986 and even though progress had been made, many people were still living in the closet; this was especially true at St. Alexander.

I so enjoyed working with the more creative and artistic boys. We could converse in my classroom about a wide range of topics. I loved it. I found that the most sophisticated thinkers would seek me out because I was willing to entertain all kinds of questions. The football coaches found it strange that so many boys spent time with me. Why weren't they on the football team? Well, when you took a closer look, then you would understand.

"Diane, look who is spending time with you," one teacher would comment.

"So what if the boys in my classroom are gay? So what?" I replied.

But I knew how to operate in two different worlds just like my students did. I was living and working within a Catholic system, yet I had undergone an abortion. I had sinned greatly, and some could even claim that my actions excommunicated me from the church. So I was teaching, attending Mass, and living a Catholic life knowing that I was one of the greatest sinners and that my deep desires for sexual expression lurked right below the surface of my existence. What was I to do? Those deep desires would surface again, but how, where, and when could I express myself?

I left St. Alexander after one school year knowing that another group of mustangs would arrive at my door come fall, and that realization disturbed me. I would also have to deal with a difficult department chairperson who would not care much for my ideas and insights.

Early on, I knew I needed support to become the teacher I wanted to be; however, I couldn't image getting the support I needed at St. Alexander. It was a male-dominated atmosphere, and there really was no place for weakness. How could I tell Harold or any of the leadership at St. Alexander what I wanted and needed? And even if I did, would the administration understand? I did not think so.

Today, I wonder what could have happened, but back then it seemed clear to me: even if I made a little bit less, I had to work in a girl's school to get the support I needed to establish myself as a good teacher.

In 1986, I didn't really believe I could dance in the classroom, but I was curious, and I wondered what would happen if I tried.

CHAPTER TWENTY-SIX

A Room Where I Could Talk About God

I REMEMBER LOOKING AT THE salary schedule. I think the salary for a second-year teacher at St. Theresa High School was $1,500 less than I made at St. Alexander. I was still living with my Mom and Dad at the time, so I didn't have to worry about rent. However, $13,500 was hardly enough to make a living.

I remember giving some consideration to public school teaching. Would I fare any better there? Unfortunately, all I knew was the Catholic system. So leaving St. Alexander for St. Theresa created a "comfort factor" for me. At St. Theresa, I would make less, but I would be in a Catholic world again surrounded by female administrators. I was hoping this would make a difference. Surprisingly, it did.

On top of all this was the opportunity to go from being an English teacher to a religious studies teacher. I was overjoyed! This time I could be in a room where I could talk about God. Yes! I could talk about God.

I never mentioned my sins and my missteps during my interview for the job at St. Theresa High, but I knew that if I got the job, perhaps that meant God did need me. I know this sounds juvenile, but in many ways I was a late bloomer. And so often when things worked well, I knew God was pleased with me, and when things didn't work out so well, I thought I had fallen out of favor with God.

I wondered if I was like the Old Testament heroes who had made really bad mistakes but then were forgiven by God. Could it be my turn? Could God have pardoned my sin? To speak on behalf of the Gospel and the Holy

Book was music to my ears. I was an ordinary laywoman who enjoyed the company of a man in a deep way, and God wanted me? Me? That $13,500 was like a gift from heaven. I could live off crumbs as long as God loved me, and he must have loved me to have provided me with this job at St. Theresa High School.

I became a different person at St. Theresa. I got involved with a number of activities, including retreats and after-school events, and I even made some good friends. Within a short time, I felt as if I was on my way to a new life and great career.

It felt so good to get my career going. I was twenty-seven by this time and well behind my classmates from Holy Jesus High School who were on to graduate school or busy having their second child. Being surrounded by young girls at St. Theresa was so much easier than working with the mustangs—almost too easy. At St. Theresa, I could smile and be myself even in the classroom. In fact, I began to notice that when I brought my whole self into the classroom things went a lot smoother. Sharing some of my personal stories with the students, when it was appropriate, often served as a great teaching tool. I often enjoyed providing an illustration by turning to one of my own challenges in life to make the point clear. I was starting to dance a little bit at this girls' school, and Room 32 seemed to be alive and well once again.

CHAPTER TWENTY-SEVEN

A Room with a Female Administrative Team

AT ST. THERESA, I BEGAN to take a good look at myself and some of my shortcomings as an employee. Yes, I was a professional, but I still had a lot to learn. I will never forget that at St. Theresa, I started to take advantage of the system. I began to take my time turning my grades into the office at the end of each grading period. It may seem like a small thing, but it was not, and my negligence was noticed by the assistant principle. She called me into her office to write me up and tell me that I had better shape up as a teacher.

This challenge was a great wake-up call for me. At St. Alexander, I was on edge, and that feeling of being on edge kept me in line. I was too afraid to make a mistake or challenge Harold or be bold in public. At St. Theresa, under the guidance of a female administrative team, I could relax. The only problem for me was this: when I am too relaxed, I just do not perform as well. Being on edge would get me to perform at the top of my game.

It is funny how I am just now making sense of these dynamics in a deeper way. Being around a female administrative team put me at ease and being around a male administrative team made me doubt myself and forced me to push myself and work hard and never let up. In a woman's world, I could be myself—whatever that meant at the time. But in a man's world, I just wasn't quite right.

Perhaps these nuances that came to the surface had a lot to do with my own life at home with my parents. My Dad, who was never satisfied with himself, went to confession each week to be pardoned for his sins, and his attitude seemed to rule our household. Dad set the tone in many ways. In fact, he was often disturbed that so many Catholics took communion on Sunday but only a handful went to confession the day before. Back then, my Dad followed many of the doctrines to the letter of the law. And, unfortunately, with my Dad, I never felt good enough. I felt that something was lacking, something had to be adjusted and better be adjusted correctly.

I didn't feel that way with my mother. With Mom, I could be more relaxed. If I made mistakes, that was just the cost of being human. For my Dad, mistakes were like some kind of blot on the record of your life. I think my Dad spent most of his life agonizing over those blots and blemishes and recounting his sinfulness, even after he left the confessional.

And for my Dad, growing to become an adult with all the trials and tribulations made life terribly problematic. That sin of Adam and Eve was real and once your innocent days of childhood were over, what could you do? For my Dad, you had to just grin and bear it, but you also had to resign yourself to the fact that sin was everywhere, and nothing would be perfect ever again. And grace didn't really mean much to my Dad; it was all about works for him. You had to work hard every day to gain God's grace, and that included weekly trips to the confessional. Sometimes I would follow my Dad's lead, and other times I would not. Sin was everywhere. How could I escape my human condition?.

One day, there was a strange turn of events at St. Theresa. The religion teachers were encouraged to talk about sexuality and birth control in their religion classes. In fact, I will never forget how awkward it was to finally have the freedom to speak about sex. Of course, with young women, it was easier to do. I had grown up with three sisters, and in some ways it was like being at home with them. In fact, being surrounded by women felt very comfortable and very familiar to me.

In many ways, the sisters who set the tone at St. Theresa Catholic High were more concerned about preserving the lives of the young women in their care then they were about preserving church teaching. I was grateful.

Being afforded the room to be a sexual being in a Catholic environment was pretty amazing for me. It was the first time in a Catholic school that I was given the space to do so. Room 32 was alive and well, and perhaps I was really living in Room 32, only this time it was disguised as St. Theresa Catholic High School so people in the Catholic community wouldn't make a fuss.

CHAPTER TWENTY-EIGHT

A Room in a Suburban Catholic School

FINDING A WAY TO SUPPORT myself on the wages at St. Theresa High School was difficult. I could relax and be myself at St. Theresa, but there would be a financial cost for this "conformability factor." Living with Mom and Dad at twenty-seven already seemed quite odd to me, especially since I was out on my own at twenty. It is funny when I think about it. I got my four year degree, but my salary after I had secured that degree didn't provide any more freedom for me. I was barely making it.

Eventually, I would make my way to a suburban Catholic school, the place where I would really develop into a fine teacher. But the transition from the south side of Chicago to suburbia was no small task for me. In suburbia, I would have to deal with a different class of people. Now I know that not everyone at Blessed Sacrament was from an affluent family, but out in Naperville, I taught students whose parents and grandparents were highly educated. Also, I had students who drove vehicles that I could only dream of driving.

How I arrived at Blessed Sacrament was not as important as how I adapted to this new environment. Moving from a blue collar environment to a white collar environment was more difficult than anything I had done up until that moment. How could I possibly teach these wealthy children? And what did they need Jesus for? If you can buy what you want when you want it, then do you need a savior? It was peculiar for me because in some ways I had to be an apologist and make a case for Christianity in a Catholic school. When I say this, I don't mean that the students at Blessed Sacrament were faithless. No! My new students at Blessed Sacrament simply had privileges I had never known before, and I wondered what I could offer these students.

In the beginning, I came off as a preacher—and not a very good one at that. I spoke about God, Jesus, salvation, and social justice, but most of the students could pick up my angry tone. Was I angry? Sure! I was thirty and just beginning to make a living wage working for a Catholic school system and teaching about social justice. I was a woman who could never be a Catholic priest speaking about how Jesus was a feminist. I was a female teacher who could never be on the administrative team because I didn't have male genitalia. But it was not like I was conscious of all this back then.

In fact, I will never forget one of my "brave" students, Jill, who stood up in the middle of class and challenged me: "How can you, an educated woman, espouse Christianity when it has not been supportive of a woman's voice or a woman's place in society?" What did I have to say? Not much. Of course, I did keep her comments in the back of my mind. However, it would be many years before I could leave Catholicism behind.

As I allowed myself to struggle and question in the presence of my students, I began giving my students the freedom to draw their own conclusions and struggle with what they had been force-fed all their lives. It was very strange, but in many ways the integration between my Catholic life and Room 32 began at Blessed Sacrament. There I started ever so gradually to develop a mind of my own. I still couldn't make any dramatic pronouncements, but I was beginning an integration process that happened because of the strength and great insights of the students in my care.

I guess I could say that I began to dance at Blessed Sacrament; it wasn't a graceful waltz, but I was dancing with my students and creating space for conversations—space I had never known in a religious education class. Those students at Blessed Sacrament were changing my life, and they were changing my destiny.

CHAPTER TWENTY-NINE
Reconsidering Jesus

As I got more comfortable with my students, with their questions and with my own life as a teacher and as a very real human being, I began to read periodicals that challenged some of the traditional thinking that was often presented in religious education classrooms in the 1990s.

I was given an article from the *Catholic World* entitled "Was Jesus a Feminist?" Sr. Mary my department chair at the time thought it might be a good addition to my class. The article was written by Leonard Swidler, and in it Swidler was raising questions about the role of women in Jesus' day and how Jesus responded. I decided to bring the article into my own religious studies classroom to see what the students would think. Perhaps it might spark a lively discussion.

After reading the article some students had questions about Jesus and his sexuality. "Ms. Banasiak, is it possible that Jesus was married? The Gospels don't speak about this, but is it possible?" asked one brave and inquisitive student.

How was I to respond in that moment? I never expected this. I thought we would simply talk about the role of women in Jesus' day. What was I to say next? I immediately thought it might be best to turn that question around. "If Jesus had been a married man, would that have made a difference? If so, then what kind of difference?" These were the best questions I could develop while thinking on my feet.

Some students loved my questions. Some wondered if Jesus had lived like an ordinary man of his day, then would that change salvation history. Would a sexually active Jesus change anything? What would change?

Many came to the conclusion that issues of sex and sexuality might be handled in a healthy manner in the modern church if Jesus had been a married man. Perhaps religious leaders wouldn't be celibate today if Jesus had not been classified as such. "Did we get the story all wrong?" some students wondered. "Have we misrepresented Jesus?" some asked. Some students even found the questions and wonderments delightful. However, there was at least one young man who was disturbed by the conversation. He wasn't sure what the point was. "Why do we need to challenge the thinking that has been established by the Catholic church?" Devin asked. "What are you trying to do, Ms. Banasiak?"

At that point, I thought I might be called into the principal's office. Devin's tone was serious, and I was challenging church thinking and church authority. However, I remember now that Devin's questions had more to do with his own discomfort about being a sexual being himself. He was not dating anyone, and he did not know how to navigate among the girls who were his peers. Life was not going very smoothly for Devin; this I knew.

As Devin questioned me that day, he appeared to be asexual, detached, and removed from his flesh-and-blood existence. Then I began wondering if many of the early church leaders at the time were not unlike Devin, holding on to thinking that didn't really serve their flesh-and-blood existence. *And what about that story of St. Origin,* I thought to myself. St. Origin had his own difficulties, and for him castration was the antidote. It appeared to me that for some of our church fathers, it was better to live as half a man than to choose a sexual and, therefore, a sinful existence.

CHAPTER THIRTY
A Room with a Good Partner and a Good Friend

Even though I started to feel more advanced and accomplished as a teacher at Blessed Sacrament, I started thinking it was time to get married and settle down. I never really stopped to ask myself if I was the marrying kind, but I did want a partner. I also thought it would be great to have my own family.

Most of the single female teachers at Blessed Sacrament wanted to get married and settle down too, but some of the single male faculty members did not think along those lines. They seemed to enjoy being single. On occasion, the male faculty members would disparage their lot as married men. I wasn't sure what the fuss was all about, but as a woman I knew I had few options.

I was getting more serious about establishing a partnership and, as a result, I spent more of my free time on my bicycle. It only made sense that I would look for a partner who might enjoy doing the things I did.

I met Lee on a ride. It was the Dog Days Double sponsored by the Oak Park Bicycle Club. I gave Lee some refreshments on his ride, and before we knew it, we were exchanging numbers and cycling together. To have a male companion was good, but to have a cycling buddy was even better. I was lucky. But along with my relationship with Lee came my relationship with Lee's family. His mom and dad were very active and involved Catholics. They spent a great deal of time doing service projects for the church and the community. Sometimes I wondered if I was drawn to Lee because of the relationship we had or because of the relationship I had with his family.

My parents never really understood my deep involvement with the church and my desire to be of service to the world, but the Lee's family did. It made sense to them.

Lee, at the time, was not really a churchgoer. Occasionally, he went with me, but he did try to avoid the things his parents enjoyed. There seemed to be some tension between Lee and his parents, and I picked that up from the beginning. I would disregard most of it, and I would recognize that most men seemed marginally religious at best.

One of the best parts about my relationship with Lee was the fact that he allowed me the space to wrestle with the difficulties of my past. Settling down meant I had to take a good look at my life, and I didn't always like what I saw. I began group therapy while dating Lee and because of that counseling, I grew in ways I had not done before.

Of course, Lee was there to hear me out and learn about my less-than-perfect life. But Lee never really judged me and always seemed to accept my insights and revelations. I was grateful for that, and I am still grateful for the friendship that developed.

My marriage to Lee was strange for me because I married a good friend. Yes, we did have a few passionate moments, and we loved each other, but I think ours was more of a good friendship that I made into something more. I asked him to marry me. And although he was surprised, he said yes. In a few months, I had a ring and we were officially engaged. How did it all happen? Was it greed or jealousy? I am not sure which. I could say that I wanted what others had; I wanted to have a partner and family, but I couldn't wait and surely felt by this time that God would not provide me with a husband. Taking matters in my own hands was my mistake. But I wanted a partner and companionship, and I just wasn't willing to let things develop naturally.

CHAPTER THIRTY-ONE

A Room at a Catholic Seminary

WHILE I WAS MARRIED, I worked on a master's degree in theology at St. Paul Seminary. It sounded so impressive to be a theologian. Perhaps my new study could wash away my sins. Perhaps I could be "made new again" with a new degree that I would obtain with the help of new and powerful teachers and mentors. But Dr. Zach Prophet, one of my professors, made a profound declaration: "Diane, once you embark on this path, you don't know what will happen. You may be transformed by this experience in ways you cannot imagine."

Dr. Prophet's words frightened me. What path was this? Would it destroy me? Did I really want to develop a new way of thinking and living? I just wanted another degree and tenure at the private Catholic high School where I was teaching at the time. What kind of journey was I on? Worse yet, could I ever turn back?

I grew at St. Paul Seminary and in my marriage in ways I didn't expect. Lee was a great blessing to me. He listened to me as I came to terms with a broken past and a childhood that was abusive. He listened as I came to new insights and new revelations. I was indeed someone who wanted to belong, who wanted to fit in. I was also someone who was still running from herself and from her past. Could I find peace? Would I? With the truth now out in the open, I could begin piecing my life back together. And with the theological language I was learning, I was given a great gift; I was given a new language system to understand sin, suffering, and redemption.

At St. Paul Seminary, I read most of the Bible and was reacquainted with biblical heroes who had their own wrestling matches with God. For instance, David, the great King of Israel, gave over to lust in his affair with Bathsheba. Yes, even David gave himself over to sins of the flesh, and he was a king!

Studying the Bible, especially the Old Testament, helped me on my journey. My ancestors in faith were not the most admirable souls. They made some terrible mistakes, yet God was calling them. And then there was Moses, the profit par excellence who was called to free his people. But if you read the story carefully, then you know that he was a murderer.

I wondered how God could call these people. I wondered if he worked with us, warts and all. Does God know who we really are and still need us? What kind of creations are we, and how can we possibly serve with so many sins that haunt us and torment us?

My graduate studies at St. Paul Seminary would help to transform me in ways I could not imagine. I was slowly starting to forgive myself for my many sins of the flesh and more willing to consider that I might have a role to play in salvation history. Perhaps I would only be a high school religion teacher, but I could teach, flaws and all, because God needed me.

CHAPTER THIRTY-TWO
A Room in Appalachia

ONE OF THE BEST PARTS about my relationship with Lee was the adventure we enjoyed together. We enjoyed some great adventures from the seat of our bicycles, and some wonderful adventures with foreign exchange students as guests in our home. We enjoyed adventures in cooking by creating interesting dinner parties and fantastic meals together. We enjoyed adventures through the wine country in California and adventures in Buenos Aires, Argentina. But our best adventure together was the creation and execution of a creative service learning trip at Blessed Sacrament High School. We created an education program that would make its mark at Blessed Sacrament and on the community as a whole.

Lee and I created a spring break service trip to Western Virginia. We took students to Appalachia to learn and grow and examine how people in a different region of the country live and work. When Lee and I began, we had support from those who had experience with this kind of service learning program, but in time, we would be on our own leading the students at Blessed Sacrament along with a few trusted chaperones.

This is when I started to believe that experiential learning was the best way to teach religious education. For me, good religious education had to inspire transformation. I knew then God was the one who transformed hearts and minds, but I wondered how I could participate as a bigger player in God's good work. Creating a dynamic educational environment allowed questions to surface among the participants, questions that might inspire people in ways I had never even imagined.

I was supported by the principal at Blessed Sacrament, encouraged to do my homework and get the necessary permission forms and parents' signatures. But other than that, I was on my own.

We would travel in vans, fifteen students and several chaperones, to Appalachia to work on small home projects in Clintwood, Virginia. We would stay in a bunkhouse, prepare meals together, and work together on different projects and worksites. At the end of each day, the group would return and gather to discuss what had gone on. In the evening, we would pray and process what the students had encountered. It was amazing. The questions that surfaced on those service learning trips were profound. Students would ask questions—many questions on these trips. "Why are these people so poor?" some wondered. "Why are the coal companies destroying the mountains and ruining the water supply?" they asked. "Why don't these people just get out and go somewhere else?" These questions made the big difference for me because I knew that Lee and I were inviting the students from Blessed Sacrament to take a look at our world in a brand new way.

Also on these trips, the students were wrestling with God and life. I could take a back seat on these trips and allow the students to draw their own conclusions. It was very freeing for me. I didn't have to worry about the doctrine or the dogma of the Catholic Church. I was simply inviting my students into an experience and then letting that experience be the teacher.

And transformations did take place on those trips! Students saw the bigger picture, and they began asking themselves questions about the connection between coal mining and poverty, substance abuse and unemployment, the loss of one's land and the loss of one's soul. In this wonderful experiential classroom, I was indeed back in Room 32 again, but this time our classroom included real-world education out in the hollers and hills of Western Virginia.

Dancing in Virginia with my husband and my students and a few chaperones from Blessed Sacrament was like heaven on Earth. The kingdom of God was real, and I was participating in it! The world was alive with majesty and wonder, and I sat back in wonderment and awe!

CHAPTER THIRTY-THREE
A Room of Body Work

AT SOME POINT, I STARTED to notice things about my body that scared me. I remember feeling as if someone had stuffed marbles down my throat and, as a result, there was a blockage. I wondered if I had a tumor and if I was developing cancer. I remember calling my friend Sister Madeleine. She said, "Diane, I think you have anger issues." Anger issues? Me?

Sister Madeleine recommended I call Brad, who was a priest and a shaman. I wasn't sure how a priest could also be a shaman, but he was. Apparently, Brad knew all about body work. He helped people to deal with their bodies and emotional lives in a dynamic and creative way.

I was afraid to work with Brad, and I couldn't get angry in front of him, at least not in the beginning. And Brad said he wouldn't work with me if I couldn't be angry. In fact, he said this: "True intimacy means that you can be real with another person, and that includes being angry with them. Choosing how to express that anger is what is essential."

I had never "danced with anger." Mostly, anger was to be avoided at all costs. Anger made a person look really weird and say things she shouldn't really say. I was angry once with my mother. Something erupted inside of me, and I said things I never should have said. I also saw my Dad get angry all the time, sometimes over the smallest of things. And when Dad would get angry, I was so frightened. He became a man I didn't like and would say and do things that were very hurtful.

I didn't want anger in my life, and I tried very hard not to let my anger show. But I am human, and anger is and was a part of my life. I just never felt safe enough to be angry. Seeing Brad meant I would take the journey back to myself by claiming and expressing my emotions, anger included.

If you tighten your first and hold it there and keep on holding it, then you will know what I felt like. My throat was "full of marbles" because I needed to express my distaste for what was; I needed to express my anger. With Brad's patience and loving-kindness, I began to express myself in ways I had never done before. In fact, I said "fuck" for the very first time in Brad's presence. Wow! That was a big step for me, and surprisingly, nothing happened. No lightening bolt. Nothing! Brad thought my dress rehearsal was a "big success." I laughed, laughed out loud for a very long time. Yes, this girl with her great smile was beginning to develop some texture and depth, and I liked it. I found such a great release working with Brad; before long, my throat was healed, and I would return to see Brad again and again.

But bringing this information back to my husband was difficult. He didn't want to work with Brad or explore his anger even though he also had some issues with it. I wanted Lee to experience what I had experienced, but he was not ready, and I started to want a companion who wouldn't always erupt in a violent outburst when things did not go smoothly.

I was dancing with anger and feeling stronger than ever. Quickly, I began to realize that I might have to continue this dance on my own.

CHAPTER THIRTY-FOUR

Spirituality in a Room at Boston College

IT WAS 1999 AND I wanted to new adventure in education. By this time I had been a religious education teacher for 10 years. I liked it, but I wanted to go deeper with my faith tradition, my prayer life and with my study. Spirituality studies seemed the next step for me, and this time my goal was to study at Boston College to pursue post graduate work in spirituality. Once accepted to the program, I would work over three consecutive summers, and I would learn about spirituality.

For me spirituality had to do with "living the faith"—making it a more personal and real, and living it every day. My theological studies had been a good for me; theology had given me a wonderful foundation in Catholicism, but I still had questions. I kept asking about our day-to-day lives. What did living daily as a Catholic Christian require? What did it mean to live the gospel? What did it mean to make my life a living prayer?

With these questions in mind, I made my application to the program at Boston College. It was my first step toward an educational experience that would take very far from home. I would be at Boston College for three consecutive summers for a two week program. I knew I would grow from this experience, but I was just not sure how I would grow.

One part of our work centered on spiritual direction. We would learn how to become spiritual companions to others. I learned that being such a companion required listening—listening to a person's heart. Listening to someone's heart was greatly appealing to me. I knew that being trained in this kind of listening would be fabulous.

We practiced this listening with each other in the classroom first. These were indeed holy moments; the spirit felt so alive and present with us, and I was hooked from the very beginning. I loved listening to what really mattered in a person's life—to hear what my classmate was saying beyond the words or through the words. In this process, I would also try to reflect back what I heard as a point of clarification. As I did, my partner during my practice session would indeed make progress. I began to wonder what life would be like if we all sat around listening to each other—if we all listened to hearts. What new information would we have about ourselves and about each other? Furthermore, why didn't heart centered listening matter much in the culture within which I lived? Could we all really get anywhere without such listening?

Another facet of my education required that we prepare and deliver homilies. I was so excited about this because I knew I could take my theological education and my role as teacher and use them together. I would explore a sacred Biblical text and then empower and inspire the community with what I had discovered. I was not sure I would be good at this enterprise, but my very first homily made a great impact on my classmates. Dale listened with great care, and afterwards he fumbled for words. When he finally settled on something, he said this:"Diane you have charisma. Your words were very moving to me. You have touched my heart." Could I be good at preaching— at preparing and delivering a homily?

At Boston College during that summer program, I prepared another homily, and during a liturgy I delivered it. I received some wonderful responses, and I was thrilled. My only questions were this: What does a Catholic lay woman do who has a gift for preaching? Where does she go? Who would hire her? And what would the Bishop say?

I learned a lot during those three summers in Boston, but mostly I learned that teaching was not my only gift. I had others. Where could I put those gifts to work? I was hopeful that I could find a way.

CHAPTER THIRTY-FIVE
Internalizing Room 32

WHILE TAKING MY SUMMER COURSES at Boston College, it became clearer to me that I needed to speak with Lee about our relationship. Perhaps I was listening to my heart. I did love Lee, but with my new experience and with new insight I realized that I had made a mistake. I had taken our lovely friendship and turned it into a martial relationship. I was not sure we had what it took to continue this journey together as husband and wife. Perhaps counseling would make this clearer for me—for us.

I am the one who initiated the conversation and then eventually the divorce. I just felt stifled and small in my relationship with Lee. We went to counseling to try to resolve things, but Lee wasn't ready to look into his past, and I couldn't move forward without him doing so. I also wanted more intimacy in our relationship; I just knew that Lee could not provide what I needed. I was listening to myself and trying to claim what was best even if it was hard to do. His comments to me as the end drew near truly amazed me: "Diane, we helped each other get to this place. We were put into each other's lives for a reason, and we got each other to a new place and a new way of thinking and living." Lee was more gentle with himself about the relationship and the ending than I was. He seemed to take it all in stride. I did not.

The divorce was the worst challenge I ever had to face. My friend was essentially gone, and I had to start over. Starting over without a lover I knew; starting over without a friend nearly destroyed me. Friendships were my lifeline, and my ex-husband and I had a friendship. We cycled across the United States, and we hosted students from around the world. We had grand dinner parties and planned mission trips to Appalachia together. It was a wonderful friendship. And most people were shocked and surprised when they heard the news. In many ways, I would say we hid things very well.

But my desire for a deep and fulfilling sexual partner remained. What can I say? The desires that first surfaced as a teen were there, and I chose to let go of a friend in search of a lover. And if that lover never surfaced, at least I would be honest. My ex-husband and I had a great friendship, but we weren't creating passonate scenes in a great love story. We were friends and not lovers.

However, once the divorce was a reality, I wasn't sure I could love a man or make love ever again. Losing Lee was terribly painful and frightening. Within a few months, I declared I would be celibate. Perhaps I just needed to let go of a sexual relationship all together. Some of my friends laughed at me, and others wondered about my declaration. "Diane, this is only temporary and things will eventually change," they told me.

Change? I was so sad about the divorce, even though I knew I did the right thing. It was hard to believe that what I was experiencing was only temporary. Could things change? In that moment, I decided to bargain with God: "God, give me a future, and I will give you my vagina!"

CHAPTER THIRTY-SIX

A Room at the Convent and
a Room to Explore

AFTER MY DIVORCE, I DECIDED to return to the convent, but this time I didn't pursue religious life. I simply decided to rent a room with the sisters until I found my way again. There was a part of me that wanted to remain with Lee and to remain a wife. There were some anger issues that lingered between us, and we didn't always have the kind of intimacy I found with therapists and confidants, but life was comfortable, safe, and predictable. However, deep within I heard this voice: "Diane, it is time to go, and you know it."

When I knew I could not live as a married woman any longer, I was angry with myself. If I had not rushed into my relationship with Lee, I would have figured out what we had and what I should do. Unfortunately, I wanted what everyone else had. And in my early thirties, I wasn't strong enough to claim what I wanted for myself. A married life seemed like the next stage in my own development. How could I deny our cultural norms and live as a single woman forever?

Furthermore, I always felt like single life was a transitional lifestyle—on the way to another vocation, either married or religious. To remain single forever seemed like a temporary kind of existence. Who remained single forever?

Also, I began to recognize that after leaving my family in my early twenties, I became a bit of nomad. Did I like this existence? Not always. Often when I discovered a new home, one that seemed "just right" for me, I thought I should stay put. After all, my Dad had the same job for more than thirty years. Why couldn't I be more like my Dad? Why was I a wandering soul?

Struggling to accept my nomadic existence has been a big part of my life's story. I knew I could stay wherever I wanted to live or work, but staying put and establishing roots until retirement often sounded like death to me. If I stayed in one place too long, then life could get boring, stale, and routine. Moving on and finding a new direction is what makes my heart sing. But after the divorce, I felt restless and directionless. Nothing seemed to fit.

One of the best things I did for myself that year was to take an Artist's Way class. It was the first time I considered myself as a creative artist. I wasn't drawing or painting things, but I would be creating a different kind of life. I thought to myself, *This is just what I need!*

In the class, we were instructed to write what are called "artist pages." This meant we were to journal for twenty minutes each morning or afternoon. I was struggling with myself again, but this time I was older, no longer married, and renting a room at a convent. Once I could get past my external circumstances, I could get to the "heart of things." What did I want for myself and where was I going?

In this class, I gave myself permission to explore other church communities. I remember going to Oak Park and worshipping at a United Church of Christ. The biggest difference was the fact that a woman was leading the service.

I was struck by powerful feelings of peace and grace in this new and different environment. With a woman leading, I felt an energy and a power I never had in the Catholic Church. What was happening to me? Room 32 seemed to be alive again yet this was a Protestant church. What did the Protestants have that we Catholics did not?

At this Protestant church, I remember reading the open and affirming statement written in the church bulletin. I found it strange and wonderful and liberating that this particular community made the declaration that everyone was welcome. Communion was for all of us. It didn't matter who you were.

Inside the sanctuary, I saw gay couples, including ones with children. This was the first time that I experienced such an open and affirming community that really practiced what it preached.

In a Catholic community, your sexuality could be acknowledged, but if you were gay or divorced, then exploring your sexuality was forbidden. Some particular Catholic communities could be accepting of people "outside the norm," but according to the Magisterium, the great teaching body of the church, sexual experimentation was strictly forbidden. One could be gay and Catholic, but to explore one's sexuality as a gay person could jeopardize one's salvation. One could be divorced, but without an annulment one would be considered an adulteress.

I wondered if I could stay in such an open and affirming community. Could I make a new home among the Protestants? A big part of me wanted to do just that. But another part felt like I had unfinished business with the Catholic church. So even though the environment at the United Church of Christ made me feel at ease, within a short time, I was back at the Catholic church, considering ministerial options. The invitation to a more inclusive vision was what I wanted, but somehow I wasn't ready to embrace that expansive vision. I also wondered if I could be the one to bring a more inclusive vision to the Catholic community. Could I help lead the way?

Room 32 was alive, but I wasn't ready to make a home in it—not with the Protestants. I felt too Catholic and too rooted to my Catholic past—in the ritual, tradition, and theology.

So I made a bargain with God: "I will serve the Catholic church, but I am giving you an ultimatum, God. I will give the Catholic church one more chance. If I can lead in this Catholic world, then I will remain a Catholic. But if I am denied a leadership role, one that I feel is growing within me, then I will leave the Catholic church behind and go in search of a new way of living and a new way of believing." I was convinced that God received my message that day, and I was hoping that God would provide.

CHAPTER THIRTY-SEVEN

Catholic Campus Ministry

It was in Kentucky that I started dancing and practicing yoga and expanding in new ways. It was amazing. Charley Harvey, a member of my dance community, said I was "blossoming in Kentucky." Yes, I was starting to "flower," and my true colors would gradually appear. My colors were soft and subtle at first and would gradually grow deeper and darker with time. No matter what, I knew this truth: whatever happened in Kentucky would be caused by my efforts. If I gave my heart and soul to this new community, I knew that new and vibrant connections would unfold!

I had left the windy city for Kentucky and work as a Catholic campus minister. I wanted to blossom, but I knew I would not become some exotic plant. I was still choosing a rather traditional role in a very conservative part of the country; I was choosing a new life in "the Bible belt." If I had been clear about what I was doing, then perhaps I would have considered a more liberal environment to express myself. I did not. I essentially left my world in Illinois for a world in Kentucky where the Catholic faith was cherished in ways I had not experienced before.

It was the deep faith of the believers at the Newman Center who made me consider the job and relocating. I was moved by the openness of the community and the love that was manifest. For me, heaven had come to Earth at the Newman Center, and I was being asked to lead.

There have been mystical moments in my life, but they have been few in number. Those days at Kentucky University were truly magical to me. I had surrendered and given up on a career at Boston College. I loved New England

and wanted to live out East, but something was happening at the Newman Center in Kentucky back in the spring of 2003; I felt needed again.

I had interviewed with the community at the Newman Center as a bargain with God: "God, I have struggled to serve this Catholic church with all of its requirements, rules, and regulations, and here is a new opportunity for me in Kentucky. I will give this church one more try, and if things don't work, then I am afraid I must move on." It was one of my most sincere prayers.

I was intrigued and delighted from the moment I arrived for my interview at the Newman Center in Kentucky. The members seemed to have a deep faith and receptiveness to God that captured my mind and heart. I received such a warm reception from the congregation, and in my interview, I was asked if I would preach once a month. I was told that as the campus minister, the students would need my guidance and support. "Diane would you be willing to preach once a month?" asked Rob in the interview. "Yes, I would love to preach!" I said with great excitement in my voice.

I wondered what was I being invited to here in Kentucky? What was happening? Why was this blessing being bestowed on me?

There had been times when I wondered about priesthood and my own call to lead a community of faith, but being a woman in the Catholic church made that thought hard to entertain. In Illinois, only the priests were allowed to read the Gospel and deliver a homily. Lay women, like me, were not given such an opportunity.

On the plane ride home, I said yes to God and this new community. They needed me, and I needed to start over. I loved the Gospel, was committed to God, and soon I would be leading a community of believers. Had God forgiven me? Was I being given a chance to start over again and make my life new?

Room 32 was alive again. The expansiveness of the new environment was amazing. And I could re-create my life. I was given a new role to play in salvation history, and I embraced it with all my heart!

CHAPTER THIRTY-EIGHT

Working with Students in Our Campus Ministry Room

AT THIS WONDERFUL NEWMAN CENTER in Kentucky, my life changed and grew in the most magnificent ways. I loved campus ministry. Why? I loved it because I could allow students to be themselves while I guided and supported them on their journey. This was a change from the classroom. In the classroom in Illinois, I felt I had to reinforce church doctrine. I had to convince my students that Catholicism made sense. In Kentucky, I did not have to convince anyone, or so it seemed. I just had to support and nourish the community—provide meals, and create liturgies and retreats while allowing the students within my care to explore and to ask questions and to weigh options.

The biggest change for me was this: I was now the facilitator of the learning. This is what I had wanted. In fact, I began to think that this was the "stuff" of good mentoring and perhaps good teaching too. If I could provide space for others to be, to learn and to grow, then I knew I would be doing my job.

Sometimes students would drop in for counseling, for guidance or a chat. Other times they would be asking for more education or more communal prayer. I could not believe what was going on here Kentucky. A whole new world and a brand new ministry was mine. I was a rich woman indeed, and this Newman Center was the confirmation of my rich life.

Simply put, I felt loved for just being Diane. The community embraced me from day one with open arms, and their love made the biggest difference. I was living and working within a sacred community that needed my gifts and talents and energy, and in return they offered me their loving hearts as appreciation.

In Kentucky in this new ministry, I enjoyed being a conduit for the spirit—listening and being present without asserting myself. If I had to be firm, I could. However, these were not high school students. These were young adults whose lives were just beginning to develop and whose careers were just beginning to take shape. I wanted to know how I could assist them on their journey. What did they need from me? How could I allow them to find their way while being there behind the scenes cheering them on?

I was living in Room 32 again, but instead of Hope leading the way, I was.

I was alive and on fire and full of possibilities. The students within my care lit a spark within me, and before long I was blazing with possibility and light and gratitude.

CHAPTER THIRTY-NINE
The Room with a Conservative Priest

During my interview at the Newman Center, I asked Father George if he would remain at the center for the next couple of years. "Father George, if I take this job, then I need to know about you and your future. I think I will enjoy working with you, but will you be moving on from this center any time soon? What are your plans?" He reassured me that he would be at the Newman Center for some time.

Within a year, Father George was reassigned. This liberal priest with whom I had the pleasure of working would be replaced, and my only question was this: who would replace Father George? I had gotten to know a few of the priests in Kentucky, so I knew I could ask around to determine what I could anticipate. When I did, I didn't like what I was told.

I have always had a very congenial relationship with my bosses. I generally got along with them and, in most cases, I enjoyed working with them. This new priest would not be like Father George. He would enforce church teaching. As long as I was able to take orders, I would get along fine with this new priest.

What did this mean for me? I knew that a change in administration could mean the end of my leadership role in Kentucky. I knew what the *General Instruction for the Roman Missal* said. I was technically not allowed to preach. Father George was bending the rules. The new priest would not do the same.

Father George was so ordinary. He did not need or want titles, and he seemed willing to minister to anyone and everyone. He loved us all. But the new priest was different. He loved titles and power and authority. I saw this attitude the moment we first met. And if you had no money, position, or power, then this new priest didn't have the time for you. That is the way it appeared to me.

From the moment I met this new priest, I knew I couldn't trust this him. He was very close to the bishop. Anything I said could be reported to the bishop. I had to follow the *General Instruction for the Roman Missal*, and if I did not, then I would probably be asked to leave.

I still remember my first day with this new priest like it was yesterday. He wanted to take me to dinner at a nice restaurant. I accepted the invitation with caution. I knew he wanted to talk about my job and what would be different under his leadership. This would be no relaxing night out on the town. Things would change under his leadership. I was scared.

That night, I was told my job would be different. I had to work for this priest and answer to him. I had to consult him on everything and anything. I had no authority, and I would never preach again.

Sometimes I wondered if my sinful choices had created this outcome. Were my worst deeds to blame for this sudden turn of events? At other times, I just thought to myself, "This is the beginning of the end, and soon I will be Catholic no more!"

Was I angry with God? Sure I was. I took a pay cut to do this work—this good work that made sense to me. I left my home and my life in Illinois as a seasoned teacher for a gamble with a new life and a new ministry. I left my home for a new world and a grand new opportunity, and what I had planned would not come true. What would I do now?

The practical matters of living and eating were on my mind. What was I to do with my graduate work in theology? Where could I go? My whole life was crumbling before my very eyes.

Luckily for me, a new job surfaced, and I could pay the bills. But when I left my ministerial position for a "closet" in a government agency in Kentucky, I felt as if I was living in *Dante's Inferno*. I had fallen so far from God and from grace that I had to spend my days in a cubby hole trying to make a living. This is when I let go of my Catholic heritage and temporarily let go of God.

Like Job in the Bible, I was being put to the test, and I decided I would not stay for the exam.

CHAPTER FORTY
Leaving the Catholic Church

As I left the Catholic church and my work at the Newman Center, my bodily needs and urges returned with such intensity that I thought I would be consumed by my desire. I kept thinking that my body was trying to make one final attempt to be "reckoned with." I heard deep within myself, "Diane, you deal with this body and deal with it now because one day you are going to have to say good-bye, and you will never have known the pleasure and fulfillment your body can bring you."

How true that was! I think I was almost fifty yet resurrecting my adolescence with a true desire to go back to Room 32 and do it all over again, but this time with Diane holding the script.

But holding the script also meant delving deep into myself. Being an extrovert, I began to realize that all my efforts to find a home came from the outside. I had sought comfort in relationships and the church and even in a marriage. I think I was looking for validation and acceptance from the outside in. I was secretly hoping that someone else could do the work for me and make it all right. I didn't see this as it was all unfolding, but in Kentucky, I started to feel more at home. I was growing in ways I had not before.

My yoga practice made the biggest difference. I had to look at myself in a mirror in a room full of strangers. Was I looking for the first time? Was I engaging with myself in a way I had not until that time? This seemed to be the case. I was coming to terms with myself, looking at myself, and being summoned to really love myself. That was hard to do especially when my body was sweaty, not as attractive as I'd like it to be, and I was in a room full of strangers, some of whom had better bodies and could fold their bodies into positions that I could only dream of doing. But with my yoga teacher and his guidance something was happening, and I liked it. Yoga slowly helped me to come to terms with myself.

Dancing was also a part of my healing journey. In the contra dance community in Lexington, I came to celebrate myself, my body, and the wonderful community of dancers who welcomed me with open arms. My dance community reminded me of Room 32. Very few dancers were practicing Christians; some considered themselves spiritual, but just about everyone claimed a bodily existence and celebrated that existence.

As I learned more and became a better dancer, I came alive in new ways. I was full of joy on the dance floor as I went from dancing partner to dancing partner. I could feel the energy between myself and a dance partner, even if the encounter was brief. We were on the dance floor to express ourselves in a very intimate and dynamic way.

Living in my home in Berea, I felt as if I was giving birth to new self, but this time I had the space to explore, to imagine, and to dream. In Berea, I began life coaching and asking questions of myself that I had not asked before. Questions of meaning and purpose kept surfacing, and my life coach really believed that I had a something grand to offer the world—the world outside the Catholic church. "Is there life outside this world I call home?" I wondered. "Can I make my way in the world without this powerful institution?" Freya, my life coach, gave me the space to explore in a way no one had done before, and she believed in me. She really believed in me.

Along my journey, I always believed that if people really knew me, they might not like me or approve of me. With Freya, things were amazingly different. She didn't want me to follow her or accept a particular doctrine. She just wanted me to realize that on my own, I had something to offer. It was as if I was being encouraged to take a big step and live my life in Room 32, and that room felt so big—so expansive!

CHAPTER FORTY-ONE

The Room with Death – My Father's Death

Unfortunately, just as I started to think I had a big, bold life and a bigger role to play in this world, I received this news from my mother: my Dad had cancer.

I had been on a dance weekend with some good friends when the call came. My friends and I had traveled to a contra dance in Virginia for a wonderful weekend of great fun and lots of good dancing. The call came when I was on the dance floor.

The news about the cancer shook me to the core. Life was just starting to feel good again even though I was working for the government, which I had never planned or expected. I had been in ministry and education most of my life. I had tried to console friends and students on so many occasions, too many to count. Now I had a father with cancer. I was deeply shaken. Where would I go? To whom could I turn to for help?

My Dad quickly decided to have the tumor in his lung removed. I wasn't convinced this was a good idea, mostly because I knew my Dad would not take the necessary chemotherapy after the surgery, and I had heard stories that once the cancer was exposed to air, it could spread and could do so quickly.

By the time I got the news, my relationship with my Dad had changed and matured. I was not happy he was depressed and still drinking, but I had decided to let my Dad live his life for himself. I would no longer be the "preachy daughter" who would try to convince her dad that he'd better shape up.

The journey to my Dad's death was so powerful for me. I had an opportunity to have several deep and meaningful conversations on that slow dance toward death. And right before the operation, my Dad gave me his blessing.

My sisters and I each went in to see my Dad right before his surgery. It was sacred and holy time. I went in to see my Dad first. I walked in with tears in my eyes. My Dad seemed so small and weak in some ways and yet larger in others. I apologized for not being a good daughter, giving him trouble, being difficult. Dad apologized, too. We cried some more, and then we hugged each other. But then he said something I will never forget: "Diane, I know you are going to make it. I really do."

All the years melted away in that moment. I felt so much acceptance and love from my Dad. He did love me, and that day he recognized my strength. Why had it taken me so long to hear these words? Why had my Dad been silent?

My Dad had always wanted a son, and sometimes I had felt that I had to be that son. I didn't deny my gender or want to be a man, but sometimes I felt I had to be strong—in fact, almost too strong. I was also stubborn. I often had to do things my way. And I must admit I wasn't your ordinary woman. I wanted to lead, but how was I supposed to do that as a woman in a Catholic world?

My father taught me to pray and took me to church. My mother considered these things important, too, but my father was my first religious education teacher. As I grew and developed into a woman, he often wondered why I took things, like our Catholic faith, so seriously.

I had to remind him with these words all too often: "Dad, you taught me to pray the Lord's Prayer. You taught me about all about God and about Jesus, and you took me to church. You laid this foundation. You taught me what should matter most." Once I finished, my Dad would have nothing left to say. He knew I was right. He had laid this foundation, and I was his first student—and a very good student at that.

After my Dad died, I felt like part of me died too. I felt restless and lost. How could I live without my Dad? If I should be in some trouble or difficult spot, I always knew I could count on my Dad to help me out. I did not take advantage of this, but it was so good to know that my Dad was always there if need be.

Now I would have to dance through life without my father. He had been my first dancing partner—and an amazing partner at that. He gave me my first dance lessons, and together we glided across the dance floor on more than one occasion. Dancing without Dad would be a bit of a challenge. But I did know that even without my Dad, I would dance again.

CHAPTER FORTY-TWO

The Room Filled with New Dating Partners

DATING IN MY MID-FORTIES WAS very different. Once I left the Catholic church and my ministry, I started to meet all kinds of dating partners. Mostly I took a date or two and then would decide what was next. Generally, there was never a next time. This time in midlife I was in the driver's seat, and I was loving it. Dan, one of my therapists, encouraged me to decide for myself who I found to be attractive. "Diane, what do you like? What kind of man would you like to date?" With Dan's word in mind, I decided I was not going to settle for anything but the best.

Some men were interesting, but there were issues that surfaced during the first meeting that made me hesitant to make another date. But this time I didn't care how they felt. This time it was really all about me. Some men were eliminated because I just couldn't imagine kissing them. Some of them were nice and good and kind to me, but they lacked substance. I remember that my friend Ann once said, "Diane, you need someone who can match your energy." Match my energy? No one could do that! So what was left for me to do?

Then my boss introduced me to Mike. He was way outside my normal dating pattern. He was a yoga teacher who took his yoga practice very seriously, and I was intrigued. On our first date, he demonstrated some difficult yoga poses. I was amazed. Also, Mike was the most physically fit man I had ever met. He not only practiced yoga, but he cycled as well and seemed to take exceptional care of his body.

Training his body and his mind were important goals, and I just knew I had something to learn from Mike. I tried to take my time with the relationship, but I had not been with a man in what seemed like forever. The night of *Ballet Under the Stars*, something changed. Mike said he loved me, and he kissed me. I was putty in his arms, and I knew I wanted to kiss him right back and to feel that deep physical connection that only lovers know.

With Mike, I struggled to return to a traditional marriage. In other words, once I fell for him and loved him, I wanted to return to the marriage relationship that I had left behind. I wanted my love to be sanctioned again. I wanted someone else to tell me, "It is okay to love again, Diane. You can have sex now!" Dating Mike was a mad pursuit to return to a traditional marital relationship even though I new that traditional marital relationship didn't feel right for me.

I had the power within to claim the truth of my life, but was I willing to use that power to assert my own authority? No one else had the power to determine my future. No one else! When I write these words, it is all so strange to me. Claiming power for myself is dangerous business. I might be misunderstood or mistreated. Staying small and enslaved to a grand list of "oughts" and "shoulds" gave me a family, a clan, a tribe. But once I would step out and assert my authority, anything could happen—anything!

I have to admit I was always afraid to assert my own power. Would the cost be too great? Would I lose friends? Would people no longer love me? These were my questions.

Today I know it is better to live as an authentic self than to live a phantom existence. But taking that leap five years ago was terrifying. I was taking a leap in a big, beautiful ballroom known as the world beyond Catholicism, and I looked a little awkward, felt a little lonely, and wondered if love would ever be mine.

Mike and I played tug-a-war for too long. We were codependent, and I enjoyed sex too much when we had it. But I couldn't allow the relationship to "just be." The funny thing is that as I started to date again after the breakup, I became more convinced that I would be celibate again or else I would find the most dynamic relationship I could ever imagine.

CHAPTER FORTY-THREE
The Presbyterian Room

ONCE I LEFT THE CATHOLIC church, I did not realize that I would be able to use my gifts and talents for ministry in a Protestant community. I thought I would need more education and another degree. Actually, it happened gradually, but I soon came to realize that Christianity is bigger than the Catholic church, and perhaps I could find a place to fit within another Christian community.

I checked out a few of the Protestant communities in Berea, and for a little while I became a Disciple of Christ. It was a great place to land because there was no creed but Christ, and that was very freeing for me. I didn't have to worry about a particular doctrine. Disciples are a varied group of Christians; I liked that. There could be great disagreements among Disciples on almost any subject. However, they were united in their belief in Jesus.

However, when you come from the Catholic church, with its great history and tradition, the Disciples can feel too loose and unstructured. In many ways, this was my dilemma. Could I live and worship and lead in this new tradition? The great theological discussions that existed in the Catholic church could be present among Disciples, but most did not worry about being labeled a heretic. Heresy seemed to be taken rather lightly.

Once I realized that I wanted something more from the community to which I would belong, I began to look at other options, and one surfaced pretty quickly at a big, beautiful Presbyterian church in Lexington, Kentucky. There was a position available for a director of Christian education, and I could apply. What would happen with my application was not clear, but it seemed that this might be my next step.

Soon after, I got the job at this Presbyterian church, and in many ways, it was very strange to me. I remember in graduate school arguing against Calvin, and now here I was serving a community of believers, some of whom believed in predestination. What was happening to me?

Well, in this wonderful Protestant community, I had a grand epiphany. I came to see predestination as a deep abiding belief that one knows where she is from and knows where she is going. I started to really believe that I came from love, and I was returning to love. Everything else in between was what we call life. Some folks do it well and others very poorly; some folks danced and others stood in one place. What became painfully clear was this: if you know where you come from and where you are going, then life can feel more settled, and you can get down to the business of real work.

In this Presbyterian community, I also started to embrace this concept of grace. We had talked about grace in the Catholic community, but now I was experiencing it in a deeper way. Perhaps it was the sermons and the lessons and the emphasis on grace that really made the difference. I don't know. What I do remember is this: I began to realize deep in my bones that it was all about grace, and somehow even with all my sins, I was okay. Working and living in a community that emphasizes God's grace was so healing for me. It was all done and completed with God in Christ. I was made new because of Jesus. The fragmented pieces of my life started coming together, and I was indeed a new creation. I felt it on the inside out.

I was essentially doing the Presbyterian dance, and I was feeling more and more comfortable in my skin, flaws and all. I was alive on this dance floor and starting to get in touch with my big, bold self, and Room 32 was alive and well too.

CHAPTER FORTY-FOUR

The Room Called Hell

I DEFENDED THE ROOM CALLED hell all my life. Hell was a reality, a state of mind, a condition and a place of punishment and torment. While teaching and working at the Presbyterian church, I kept my hands wrapped tightly around this concept known as hell. Had I done all the research about this teaching? Did I know enough about church history? I did not. But what I can say is this: I believed in hell, and I defended the concept quite emphatically.

However, one day in my Christian education class, a parishioner named Gregg talked to me about his beliefs. He claimed there was no place where God didn't exist. I still remember his words: "Diane, if God is tied to existence and God is the author of existence, then there is just no place where God does not exist."

What was this man saying? He was making a case for God's existence that was much bigger then my concept of his existence. Could God really be that big, I wondered? I wasn't sure. I wasn't convinced.

It was then that I started arguing with Gregg: "Gregg, we are free, and we have choices, and we can choose an eternity without God," I said emphatically. I had to make sure Gregg realized that much of our future was really in our hands.

Gregg wasn't concerned about freedom or free will; he was concerned about this expansive love of God. How expansive was this love? Had I been reducing God all these years? Was God everywhere? Did hell exist?

I began to realize that I couldn't just quote a passage in a text—a Christian text—to convince Gregg of the error of his ways. Gregg had a bigger consciousness, and church teaching wouldn't reduce his thinking, not a bit.

It was this expansive vision that an ordinary parishioner presented to me on an ordinary Sunday that has made all the difference. His thinking has stayed with me and has transformed me these past few years.

Today, I believe Gregg is right. God is everywhere. And quite frankly, I don't think hell exists anymore. I believe that hell was just something presented to church members to keep us in line and in the pew. Once I let go of hell, then I could get down to the business of real living. And if I didn't have to fear punishment and hell, then how did I want to live this life? How did I want to live in the here and now?

It took time to release the concept of hell completely. My fists were always wrapped tightly around hell's door. I had held on to hell because I feared God and feared judgment. But most of the judgment—in fact, just about all of the judgment—came from me. Letting go of hell meant letting go of judgment. That was even harder to do. It still is.

But I believe now more than ever that once life in this realm is over, I will move on to another realm, some other kind of existence, and there is nothing to fear—nothing at all. I feel wrapped in this big, thick blanket of God's love, and it often seems that this thick blanket of God's expansive love is the only thing I really want to celebrate.

God is everywhere. What I mean by God is hard to define. But I do believe I came from love, and I am going back to that love and so is everyone else. There is no need to use fear to speak about God. In fact, in God there is no fear.

Dancing without a room called hell was really bizarre. Giving up that old belief was not easy to do, but as I did, I felt even bigger and better than I ever felt before. Room 32 was growing. It was no longer just a part of me. That love and expansive vision I experienced in my high school drama room in Chicago many years ago was starting to seep into my reality. Heaven was coming to Earth, and I had nothing to fear!

CHAPTER FORTY-FIVE
The Room with Many Avatars

AT THE PRESBYTERIAN CHURCH, I had the opportunity to teach and organize adult education programming. This was the part of the job I enjoyed the most. It was exciting to develop creative programming for the members of this church community. It was how I could put my creativity to work on behalf of the community.

In the spring of 2009, I got an idea. I was considering a world religions seminar for our church. It would be a series of talks held on Wednesday nights to educate the members about different religious traditions. I was hoping this might spark some creative dialogue and greater understanding among members and those from outside our community. The idea was approved by the leaders at the church, and I quickly got to work.

I began to find leaders in Lexington and Richmond who could help introduce our members to other religious traditions. Some were practitioners of a particular tradition and others were scholars and academics. All of them did a wonderful job outlining their own particular tradition.

However, the one I enjoyed the most was the one who covered Hinduism. I can still recall the professor's words when he spoke about Hinduism: "Hinduism's challenge to Christianity is this: why only one avatar?" I remember his words vibrating in the room and in my mind. Why only one avatar? Why only one, I asked myself? This idea began to circulate within me the way the smell of coffee circulates throughout the house when it is brewing in the morning. That was it, I thought to myself. Why only one?

There have been times throughout my religious development when I looked at the prophets, both living and dead, and wondered was Jesus the only one who had been sent to us by God? Have others been sent? Could they have had just as much authority and power as Jesus? Could these others, such as Dr. Martin Luther King Jr. and Mahatma Gandhi be avatars too? I wondered. Listening to the presentation on Hinduism was one of those times when I wanted to probe a little deeper and examine these ideas some more.

When our speaker finished his presentation, I was ready to sign up for Hinduism 101. Well, not exactly. But I did wonder how I could return to the pew with this idea and newfound curiosity. I believed in the incarnation— the God made flesh story. Why? It just made sense to me. It made sense that people like Jesus were expressions of God in physical form.

But as my faith began to grow and morph, I often wondered what if all of creation was filled with God. What if God was everywhere? And what if, for me, following only Jesus made God seem too limited and just too small?

Some of my questions might not make sense to the traditional believer, but they made sense to me. And from that moment on, I wondered if I would start to dance with the world. Could I? In some ways, I wanted to, but it wasn't the right time.

CHAPTER FORTY-SIX

The Room Where I Was Able to
Think for Myself

AT LEAST ONCE IN A lifetime, there is that chance you will meet someone who can change your life for the better in the most dynamic way. I met that person a few blocks from home in a big, beautiful mansion in my neighborhood. It is funny how sometimes the best gifts and blessings can be found right in your own backyard. I was grateful!

I met Olaf in January 2009. Our first date was at Common Grounds coffee shop, and that is where the magic began. I can't tell you all the details of that first conversation, but we sat there and talked for almost three hours. I was hooked. I had never met a man who liked to converse about all kinds of deep matters—someone who really liked to "mull things over."

On our second date, I asked him about his fears. He told me about his fears without even blinking an eye. I never saw this kind of strength from a human being before. I knew it was a bold question, but I had to know.

Our adventures were many and varied; they can't be summed up in this one chapter. However, within those adventures I found a man who could truly think for himself. Yes, he grew up as a Christian, but he had questions and he hadn't always accepted the answers he was given. But it wasn't just listening to him that made the difference for me. For the first time in my life, I could think any thought, and it was welcomed like the way you welcome a friend whom you haven't seen for years but who loves you just the same.

For the first time, the door to my mind was unlocked. It was finally free. I was free! Free! To think any thought, to ponder any idea was the best gift anyone had ever given to me, and I had so many thoughts. Did Jesus really suffer and die for our sins? Furthermore, did I need to worship this Jesus? Was this what life, my life, was all about?

With Olaf, I allowed myself to let go in ways I never had before. My mind, which had been imprisoned for years, was finally free. The only problem for me was this: once any idea was welcome, then in time, I knew some ideas just had to go.

Sacrificing myself to a God started to sound like some ancient ritual that I had to relinquish. What was I doing giving my life over to Jesus? Were we, human beings, really it? Were we the God made flesh in this time and in this space? Were we the grand creations? I wondered.

Olaf articulated that idea first, and initially I thought he was crazy. I still can hear him say, "I am the way, the truth, and the life." He quoted from the Bible that day, but I knew as he did that he was not referring to the transcendent God or Jesus either. Olaf's wonderful thought started to work its magic in me.

This relationship was starting to have a profound effect in my life and in my work at the church. What was I doing there? What was I saying? Did I believe all of "this stuff" anymore? Once I started to live from the inside out, then I knew I would have to make a change in a big way. My biggest dilemma would become this: how could I remain in the Presbyterian church if I no longer really believed in the doctrine and the dogma (the suitcase) that I had been carrying around with me my entire life. That large suitcase of worn-out beliefs was heavy, and I carried it wherever I went. I also started to wonder if I let that suitcase go, where would I reside? Christianity was starting to lose its power over me. I knew I could not stay.

Finding other ways to make a living would be hard for me. After all, my master's degree was in Catholic theology. How could I get work outside the church and be paid well? What did I have to offer?

My meeting with Olaf changed everything about me—my life and my life's work. I had to say good-bye to the Diane I once knew, the church girl who dutifully sat in the pew week after week repenting for being "just Diane." I had to leave the pew with thoughts of smallness and sacrifice for a world in which I would start to claim my power, my own majesty, and my own truth in big, bold ways. I started thinking that perhaps I was the "light" sent from above to change the world. So what could I change? What difference could I make in this time-space reality? And how?

Dancing with my questions and with what I like to call my "bigness" was the greatest gift of my friendship with Olaf. And once I began dancing in this big, bold way, then Room 32 no longer was just a part of me—Room 32 was me!

CHAPTER FORTY-SEVEN
The Room with My New Business

I STARTED TO CONSIDER THE possibility of leaving the Presbyterian church. The work was good, but I could no longer embrace Christianity the way I had when I was a child. It was time to move on. When this realization hit me, then I knew I would have to find another job. But what should I do next?

The decision to start my own business developed as I considered the idea of being a life coach. In many ways, I had been coaching all my life but without the title or the credentials or the home office space. In fact, I had worked with students most of my life, and I had coached students outside of my classroom regarding all kinds of issues. I coached some of them regarding relationship issues, family challenges, and what to study in college. I also noticed, as I looked back at my life, I had always been trying to encourage people in a positive way. I had actually started with my own family members.

I began to think that if I developed a website and some business cards, got a little training, and let friends and family members know I was open for business, people would find me. So, within a short time, I gave my notice at the church and started to make plans for a new life as a business owner.

It was so exciting to get my website off the ground and to hold my business cards in my hand. The website was beautiful and so were my cards. Purple was a prominent color on both my cards and my website, and it was so much fun to see my new business start to take shape.

I also knew I could get part-time work at the university, and that would help me as I got started in coaching. By teaching a couple of classes, I thought I could strike a balance between my own work as a life coach and work as a part-time teacher. I had things all lined up that fall of 2010. Soon I would be working outside the church in ways I had never dreamed possible.

I got my training through the Coaches Training Institute. They do a fantastic job, but the classes were not cheap, and unfortunately I had not saved the kind of money I needed to save to get my training and my new business off the ground. In my naïve moments, I thought things would just fall into place.

What I discovered over time was that I had to believe in myself and my own abilities as a coach first. I would really have to believe people would give me money for my time and expertise. This was a dramatic shift for me. I had always been paid by other organizations and institutions and often by churches. Did I really think I could get paid all on my own?

At first, I realized I was looking for clients to validate me, to say "Diane, you are good. I want to hire you." Without that internal belief system in place, I would spend the next two years doing more work as a teacher than as a coach.

However, within a year and a half of doing workshops and presentations and getting the word out into the community, something happened. I suddenly believed that I had something to offer. I knew this was my calling, but I just had to wait for the clients to show up.

Eventually, they did. And as I started coaching and working with my clients, I noticed that they had so much to offer the world and me. Sure they came for guidance, support and accountability, but they also were teaching me about courage, and determination and the desire to let go of what was in order to make room for what is.

Today, I still teach quite a bit, but I also have clients and that feels so good. I am working for myself, not for the church, and I am just being Diane. In my practice as a life coach, I am using tools and tips that I have learned throughout my life. They help to guide and support my clients on their journey, but I am doing it as Diane, a business owner.

Finding the confidence and the belief in my gifts, talents, and abilities was and still is hard to do at times. There are days when I get up and wonder what I am doing. Some days everything doesn't fall in place the way I would like it to. Some days are ordinary, and I am not as energized as I would like to be. But I do believe that because I have weathered a few storms and have found my own voice, I can encourage others to do the same.

The key ingredient for me in my work is this: I believe my clients have the wisdom within. They have all the answers within themselves. I am just there to support my clients on their own inner journey, but they must do the work. I am not a savior or the one who can fix it all. I am just Diane who wants to listen and learn, support, and dance with my clients in the moment.

Dancing with my clients is so wonderful; staying in the moment the key. And perhaps what I am learning through all this is compassion and attention for what shows up. My business is a heart-centered business, and with an open heart and a willing spirit, I watch transformations take place right in front of me.

It is a pretty amazing life!

CHAPTER FORTY-EIGHT
The Room Called Ahava

WHEN I STARTED MY OWN business I also started reading books by Esther Hicks. She is a amazing women who channels the wisdom of "Abraham" into this time space reality. What Abraham encourages us to do is to pick and to choose the life we want—the life we desire. I couldn't believe there was a voice in this world encouraging me to seek out my desires—to move in the direction of my own happiness.

Once I left the Christian church, I found a freedom to expand and explore and to read things I never would have read before. People like Hicks really helped me to rethink my life, my religious beliefs and what I wanted now. I never realized that I could have whatever I sought in this life. I never fully understood that what came about did so because I first had a thought and eventually that thought became reality.

So what were my thoughts? Well, for one thing, I had been barely making it financially. Oh, I had a lot of nice things, but money didn't just materialize in my life, and my work didn't seem to generate the kind of income I really needed. Yes, I was taking care of my bills, but that was about it. If I wanted to travel, then I would have to do so with rapid reward credits on Southwest Airlines. If I wanted a new outfit, then often I had to go to the consignment stores to put one together. I didn't mind this, but I was always struck by the fact that other folks had vacation after vacation, and I was lucky if I had one vacation a year.

I was not resentful about all this, not in the Christian world. After all, I was holding on to the "church girl script," and church girls don't exactly make the big bucks. But after I left the church, I knew I wanted more.

There was a part of me that felt guilty about wanting more. I hid that secret too—at least I think I did. I didn't want to sound greedy, but I did want to travel and study some more and give gifts to people along my path.

A friend encouraged me to check out a new spiritual community in Lexington called Ahava, which is the Hebrew word for love. I had never heard of a place like that before. I wondered what this spiritual center was all about.

Soni Cantrell, the minister at Ahava, is a passionate leader. The day I came for a visit, she sang songs and delivered messages and said prayers with great enthusiasm. In fact, I was not sure whether I had ever met anyone quite like her before. And when she spoke, she did so with honesty, humility, and grace, and I was moved.

I still remember that first day like it was yesterday. The community was singing about the goodness of God with what sounded like one voice and one mind and one heart. It shook me to the core! And within a short time, tears came to my eyes. There was just something about the energy in the space and the faith of those gathered at Ahava that made all the difference to me.

Soni said that everyone was welcome—everyone. That was music to my ears. But I had to admit that I needed to test out those words for myself. Could this message be real, I wondered? But as I listened to Soni that first day, I could tell that everyone was welcome even if they had other faith traditions or other spiritual practices.

The language at the service moved me. This was a community founded on principles from Science of the Mind. What was this religion? Who was their founding father? Where could I go to learn more? Was this Science of the Mind philosophy worth exploring?

I don't feel like I can sum up Science of the Mind for you, but I can say the day I attended Ahava, the community was talking about abundant living and abundant thinking. Could it be true, I thought? Abundance, that is what I want too.

Before that day, I never realized that everything starts with me and where I am. If I feel limited or lacking, then that is what shows up. But if I feel big and prosperous, then prosperity shows up.

What I began to learn was this: the universe works by principles and that what we think comes about. And the more I began to contemplate this reality, I began to realize it was true. When I wanted to do something and I put my attention on it, then it became a reality.

I began to take a magnifying glass to examine each of the chapters of my life. How true it was. Everything I wanted seemed to come about: a college degree, a relationship, a life as a campus minister, or a life as a contra dancer. Whatever it was that I wanted seemed to be manifest.

So these days I have been thinking about abundance. I realize I do have a rich life. I have been to places some can only dream about, and I have had jobs and opportunities that some of my friends and family members cannot quite understand. I have hosted exchange students from around the world, and I have gone to visit at least one of those former students. I have cycled across the country and all throughout Kentucky, and through it all, I have been creating my life, chapter by chapter, piece by piece. Through it all, I have been finding my way to a bigger way of thinking and a bigger way of living. Through it all, I have been growing in the most amazing ways.

What I inherited as a child is not mine anymore. I outgrew the doctrines and the dogma of Christianity the way I outgrew my favorite pair of jeans or my favorite childhood hiding places. Today, I realize that outgrowing stuff is just normal. We all change and grow. This new Science of the Mind thinking and living was something I could not pass up—and I did not.

I write these final chapters as a participant in the Foundations class at Ahava. In this class, I am learning the foundations and trying to determine if Science of the Mind is the place for me. Right now, I think I have found a new spiritual home, and it feels really good, and I am very grateful. However, what will be born from this moment, only time will tell.

In many ways, I feel like I am dancing with the whole universe. My consciousness is evolving and changing and growing in this time and in this space. And even though this dance can overwhelm me at times, it makes me realize just how rich I am. I am part of this amazing, eternal, and ever-expansive dance, and it feels so good!

CHAPTER FORTY-NINE
A Room with More Work to Do

THESE DAYS I OFTEN FIND myself saying, "I love my life!" And I must admit, I truly do. However, my life as a Polish-Catholic girl from the south side of Chicago is still with me. It will never leave me. It is part of who I am. And most days I am just fine with that.

But these days I also am more aware of myself as the author and creator of my life, and I am, indeed, gliding across the dance floor in ways I never imagined. I am dancing through life and loving it.

However, even with my newfound freedom and this large and creative sense of myself, I still have work to do. In the course of writing this book, I have become painfully aware of my workaholic tendencies. I use work to cover things up. Am I embarrassed about my addiction? At times I am. But this is the way I escape the pain, the worry, the loneliness. It is my drug of choice.

Some days I am good at stopping to see what is brewing within me, and other days I just keep on working and spinning and wondering why my life seems so complicated. Often, I make my life complicated. I take on more and more responsibilities to assure myself I am good enough.

Am I good enough? Some days I think so. Other days, I am not so sure. But I am still grateful for the journey, my friends, my companions, and my family members who remind me that just being Diane is all that really matters.

I am returning to my spiritual practices with a deep desire to take time each day to sit and meditate and "just be Diane." These practices are very nourishing for me. I need rest, and I need care. My mediation and my yoga are the spiritual practices that ground me, center me, and remind me that I am good enough. Morning affirmations also make a big difference too. When I recite powerful affirmations, I am reminded of my gifts, my talents, and everything that I have to offer this world. It makes a big difference for me.

So what else can I say? Well, I am a teacher, a life coach and the creator of my life. But I am also a human being who gets afraid and lonely. I am a human being who gets confused and lost. I am a human being who wonders how many times I must let go of what was to make room for what will be.

I am no guru. I never wanted to be one. I am just a human being who has found her voice and her power and her Room 32—someone who wants to keep on making contributions in this time and space. I want to keep on making contributions until this journey ends.

Thank God for Room 32, for creative places and people who teach us to dream and create and wonder and who allow us to ask questions—any questions at all. This is the "stuff of life"—the stuff of heaven on Earth. And because heaven is here and now, because heaven has come to Earth, I know I have nothing to fear and neither do you!

Epilogue: On the Way to Enlightenment

On the way to enlightenment I recognize
Bits of glass, broken promises, and memories
Too painful to describe.

Years of running couldn't hide the truth—
The truth of what was, what is.
So how can I claim enlightenment?

All I can do is notice what happens
When your story takes me back in time.
All I can do is to observe the sensations that come,
The reactions that appear I my mind.

It is in the noticing that I have found freedom
For the demon no longer lurks at my door.
The demon, no long the "other," no longer outside myself.

The monster is a memory I cannot forget.
A child who couldn't speak out and speak up.
A child who allowed what was to shape her destiny.
Who couldn't, just couldn't say no!

So, I will sit here awhile and hold you.
I will sit here awhile and cradle you.
I will sit here awhile and love what is.

"What is" had brought me to this marvelous place.
"What will be" can take me to some place brand new!

A Special Word of Thanksgiving

It is hard to capture on paper all the people who have helped to shape me, support me, and encourage me to be Diane. There are too many to count. However, I wish to take a few moments to name those special individuals who have made my life so remarkable—a life worth living.

I want to thank my parents, Bernard Banasiak and Madeleine Banasiak. They said yes to me and my life the day I was born, and even though I often challenged them, confused them, and asked too many questions, they did a great job loving me.

I also want to thank my sisters, Karen, Susan, and Janice, for being my first companions. I have so many happy childhood memories with my sisters. We had so much fun playing together as children, and I was glad to have my sisters share the journey with me. I am grateful for them—their love, support, and encouragement.

I also want to thank all my teachers. I followed them into a profession that has sustained and nourished me in so many ways. As a teacher, I learned how to dance, how to create, and how to support young and fragile minds. I discovered my vocation because of all the many wonderful teachers who made an impact on my life.

I want to thank my drama teacher for her time, attention, and for her dedication to Room 32 and to all of us who sought out Room 32 as a home, a safe haven, a place to dream and to wonder. Hope is an amazing human being. Hope taught me how to create, to dream and to wonder.

I am grateful for my therapists, coaches, and friends who mentored me along the way. Special thanks goes to Asmund, Don, Freya, Lani, Marge, Marie, Matt, Marianne, Susanne, Pat, Rhonda, Stephanie and Lee. They have been companions on my journey; they encouraged me to keep dreaming and to keep reaching for the stars. I also want to thank Dan and Beth Hans. Dan is an extraordinary minister and a great friend who has helped me to understand that we are human beings first and ministers second. Beth is a creative and talented woman who has inspired me on more than one occasion; I appreciate and value her artistic vision. My sister Janice Rosero needs to be on this list too. She is not only my sister, but she is my friend. She encouraged me to keep on living my dream. I could always count on Janice and that made a big difference for me. All of these companions kept believing in me when I could not believe in myself. They have had a big role in the creation of my project. I am ever grateful.

Asmund Vego has been my partner and good friend for over 4 years, and his love and friendship has made a big impact on my life. Asmund kept on encouraging me to write, to share my story and to create a big, bold life for myself. I am not sure if I would have finished this project without his efforts. His love sustained me and helped me to persevere in difficult and dark times. He is an extraordinary man, a great leader, a loving father and someone who has changed my life in many wonderful and marvelous ways.

I also am grateful to Paul Sanders, my writing coach, who encouraged me to write and who supported me along the way as I composed Room 32. Paul is am amazing coach and someone who understands the writing process. He did an wonderful job stretching me and encouraging to just be Diane.

I am also grateful to the Catholic church and the Protestant church and to the many believers within those institutions who often reminded me about the vastness of God's love. Often I would forget, but good church people would remind me over and over again. God's love is so expansive. This is what I know to be true!

I owe much gratitude to Toby Traylor, Lisa Miller, Joel DiGirolamo and Jodi Chmielwski. These spiritual souls and yoga teachers helped me to deepen my spiritual practice, and they encouraged me to trust my deepest self.

Grace has to be on my list as well. She held my hand in my darkest hour. She gave me comfort and asked for nothing in return. Grace, I thank you from the bottom of my heart. You have given me a new understanding about my vocation in this world. May I be as generous with my life as you have been with yours!

Finally, I am grateful for Ahava and the teaching known as the Science of the Mind. This new spiritual community and this spiritual teaching are making a big difference in my life. I have enjoyed taking the Foundations class, and I hope to take other classes soon.

Life is a mystery, but along the way there are angels sent to guide us, love us, and help us find our way. The above acknowledgments underscore these the angels in my life. I want to honor them by name. I am a rich woman indeed!

About The Author

Diane Banasiak is a teacher, speaker and life coach in Lexington, Kentucky. Diane uses her dynamic energy and great listening skills to motivate university students and to support her clients as they make important transitions in life. She believes that everyone can have a rich and fulfilling life, but in order to have that rich life we must make choices. Clarity is what Diane can offer her clients, and over time her clients get a clearer picture of what they want and who they want to become. Diane has her own coaching business here in Lexington, and she can be found on the web at **www.justdiane.com**.

In her free time, Diane enjoys quiet times with her partner and friend Asmund Vego, cycling adventures all around Kentucky and a vibrant yoga practice.

CPSIA information can be obtained at www.ICGtesting.com
Printed in the USA
LVOW072038110313

323738LV00003B/10/P